TWANG!

RAYMOND OBSTFELD
AND SHEILA BURGENER

THE
ULTIMATE
BOOK OF
COUNTRY
MUSIC
QUOTATIONS

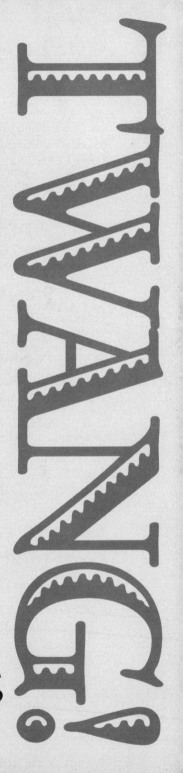

Henry Holt and Company, Inc.
Publishers since 1866
115 West 18th Street
New York, New York 10011

Henry Holt® is a registered
trademark of Henry Holt and Company, Inc.

Published in Canada by Fitzhenry & Whiteside Ltd.,
195 Allstate Parkway, Markham, Ontario L3R 4T8.

Library of Congress Cataloging-in-Publication Data
Obstfeld, Raymond, date.
Twang!: the ultimate book of country music quotations / Raymond
Obstfeld and Sheila Burgener. — 1st ed.
p.   cm.
"An Owl book."
ISBN 0-8050-4888-X (alk. paper)
1. Country musicians—United States—Quotations.   I. Burgener,
Sheila.   II. Title.
ML3524.O27   1997   97-5464
781.642—dc21   CIP
                           MN

Henry Holt books are available for special promotions and premiums. For details
contact: Director, Special Markets.

First Edition 1997

Designed by Debbie Glasserman

Printed in the United States of America
All first editions are printed on acid-free paper. ∞

10 9 8 7 6 5 4 3 2 1

For my brothers and sisters,
and for the music that accompanied
the story of our lives.

—SHEILA BURGENER

CONTENTS

FOREWORD
BY PATTY LOVELESS

Country music has always been about real life. I think it's because the artists who make it come from places that are so close to the heart of where real life happens. And it's the way they look at what happens around them, and to them that defines the things they want to sing about.

I know when I'm looking for songs to sing, I always want to find something I've either experienced myself or witnessed. When I was singing around various places before I had my record deal, people would come up to me and tell me their stories. So you can learn a lot about life making music that makes people feel so much about their own lives.

Indeed, you not only learn a lot about how people live their lives and respond to different things, you begin to learn a lot about yourself, too. Maybe that's what makes country singers so wise—and so willing to sing songs that dig a little deeper into the way we live our lives and the crosses we choose to bear.

Making music is a gift. When you have it, you take it very seriously. I know I want the songs I sing to speak to people in a way that makes a difference. I hope they feel better about something bad or understand more about what's happening in their lives or even just smile and have a good time listening to my music. When I was growing up, that's what music did for me, and I'd like to think I can pass that on.

A lot of the other country artists I know feel exactly the same way about this exchange. And being so committed to music, that dedication can't help but filter into the way you look at life. It starts defining how you look at everything, which is a pretty wonderful thing.

There's nothing like listening to country people talk. Simple. Direct. To the point. It's about getting to the core of the person, event, or problem. It's the straightest line between two points, and there's absolutely no chance of getting lost.

And this book represents a collection of the best wisdom and wit today's country stars have to offer. They're talking about all the different facets that make up the music, the business, the fans, and the people who make this music great. In a few lines, Vince Gill, Marty Stuart, Pam Tillis, and many, many more boil it all down to the essence of the truth.

For in the end, that's what it comes down to: honesty. There's no one more honest or true than a country singer. *Twang!* represents the best of the lot, talking about the things that matter to them with the kind of candor that's always let them touch people across the country.

Now it's your turn to enjoy what my friends have to say.

"Twang" is real simple. "Twang" is a square-dance caller. "Twang" is Dwight Yoakam on a jukebox in a pool hall. "Twang" is Roy Acuff singing "The Great Speckled Bird." So simple that even the smartest person in the world can understand it.

—PAM TILLIS, 1996

INTRODUCTION: THREE CHORDS AND THE TRUTH

There's an oft-repeated legend about country music. According to this legend, Japanese soldiers taunted U.S. Marines in the Pacific during World War II by broadcasting the following chant from their ships: "To hell with Roosevelt! To hell with Babe Ruth! To hell with Roy Acuff!" The idea was to destroy the morale of the American sailors by damning the most sacred of American institutions: democracy, baseball, and country music. Roy Acuff's name may not be in the history books, but his portrait belongs in the echoing halls of American tradition. His music, country music, is the soundtrack that accompanies the struggles, triumphs, and tragedies of the average American's daily life.

Country music is *our* music. It belongs to America. It originated in the backwoods of America's South, in the clear streams that run through the Appalachian Mountains, in the lullabies mothers sang to their sleepy children. And country music always acknowledges where it came from, proudly, defiantly, sweetly. It strums some integral, pure chord within us, an innocent part of ourselves that somehow remains protected from the complexities of the outside world. When we hear Bill Monroe's mandolin, we can't help but tap our feet. When we listen to Patsy Cline falling to pieces, we can't help but get a little misty-eyed.

Even in its outward simplicity, country music encompasses a panorama of sounds and styles. It can be traced back to folk tradition, can be linked to African-American blues, can even be held partially responsible for the birth of rock 'n' roll. After all, Elvis's blue suede shoes were first worn by Carl Perkins. The crossover appeal of country is finally being recognized. Today, you can hear country music pouring from car radios in the most desolate of West Texas towns, as well as on star-studded Sunset Boulevard. Garth Brooks is up there on the charts right next to Snoop Doggy Dogg and Pearl Jam. As country music expands and commingles with other styles and artists, it continues to reinvent itself, while at the same time maintaining the backwoods roots that make it an essential ingredient in our American heritage.

Hillbilly, right-wing, sentimental. Country music has been called all of these things, and more. This book will challenge any preconceptions and oversimplifications that country music critics and fans alike may share. Bluegrass musicians may be settin' on bales of hay, but they can express the power of music more eloquently than any scholar. Country songwriters may praise the institutions of God, dear sweet Mama, and the flag, but they've also written classic songs of protest, like "Sixteen Tons" and "Harper Valley P.T.A." Country singers may be crying into their beers, but you have to admit, there *is* a natural ache in their voices. Someone once asked Hank Williams why his songs were so sad. "Well," he responded, "I suppose you just might call me a sadist." Listening to his music, you just have to believe he's seen heartbreak up close.

We believe the country performer because country music is the truth. That's what its singers and musicians and songwriters will tell you again and again. It's the truth, backed by three chords. This book quotes hundreds of members of the country establishment saying just that, and much, much more. We scoured magazines, newspapers, TV specials, biographies, autobiographies—every source imaginable—searching for these singers' versions of the truth. Here, we've captured their views on fame and religion, their confessions of addiction, their philosophies on life. (Note: Whenever possible, we've included the date the quote was spoken or published; occasionally, dates were unavailable.) What they say may provoke you, make you laugh, anger you, move you; it will certainly surprise you. You've heard their songs; now listen to what these American storytellers have to say once the music stops.

It took us two years to write this book, and we could've kept going for another two years, five years, even ten. The bounty of country music is inexhaustible; new talents continue to surface, familiar faces reappear, and they always have a viewpoint to share with their fans. "To hell with Roy Acuff!" It didn't stop us back then. As long as Americans are falling in love, fighting with their fists, and two-steppin' on Saturday nights, they'll be singing and playing country music. You can count on it.

TWANG!

THE MUSIC
&THE
TRADITION

WHEN YOU'RE LOOKIN' AT ME, YOU'RE LOOKIN' AT COUNTRY

My name may be in big lights, but it's still spelled country.   —LORETTA LYNN, 1978

There are two things I won't argue about, because you can't change people's minds. One is the Bible, the other is country music.

—RALPH EMERY, radio personality and host of *Nashville Now*, 1994

If you talk bad about country, it's like saying bad things about my momma. Them's fightin' words.   —DOLLY PARTON

It is as fundamental as sunshine and rain, snow and wind and the light of the moon peeping through the trees. Some folks like it and some dislike it very much, but it'll be there long after you and I have passed out of this picture for the next one.

—GEORGE HAY, original Grand Ole Opry host, circa 1920

I think [country music] feeds us in a way that we desperately need. I believe that music is a real, positive, life-changing thing that is as necessary to the quality of life as things like food and shelter.   —EMMYLOU HARRIS, 1993

I can remember hearing songs on the jukebox, even at three or four years old, and I had an understanding of something I'd never been able to understand before. That's part of what country music does. It can make you feel right at home, or it can take you a thousand miles away.   —MARK COLLIE, 1996

I think the thing that makes country music so popular is the same thing we loved about cowboy movies. The western movies. It's like the natural heroes of the earth. There's something about the dirt, something about the horse, something about the land, something about the honesty, something about the music.

—DOLLY PARTON, 1996

I think more people are likin' the country music, and other kinds, too. They like the rock, you know, but you still get a hell of a yell out of 'em when you go out there and do a good ol' country ballad.

—GEORGE JONES, 1988

There is a pulse of the people and what they want. I trust the people; I really do. I think if good music is made available to them, they will be drawn to it. . . . Now I believe there will always be an audience for pure country music . . . and even if there isn't, I'll still be singin' it.

—EMMYLOU HARRIS, 1993

> I'M A GREAT NOSTALGIST. THAT'S KIND OF MY DEPARTMENT, TENDIN' TO THE ROOTS OF COUNTRY MUSIC. AND I'M DOING EVERYTHING I CAN TO PRESERVE WHAT I KNOW.
>
> —MERLE HAGGARD, 1996

You can't be fish and fowl; up in New York they say country music's on the pop charts now, but you can't be country and be on the pop charts at the same time. . . . When I'm talking to an artist or a writer about coming with us, I want to know where he was born; if he was born in New York, he'd have to have an inoculation to know country music.

—WESLEY ROSE (1918–1990), head of Acuff-Rose Publications

I hate to see country music going uptown because it's the wrong uptown. We're about to lose our identity and get all mixed up with other music. We were always a little half-assed anyway, but a music dies when it becomes a parody of itself.

—CHET ATKINS, 1976

Some people never want country to try anything new. Thank God Buck Owens plugged in a Telecaster [guitar] and helped them get over it.

—KIX BROOKS, of Brooks & Dunn, 1996

This is not your father's country music anymore. But it's getting harder and harder to figure out just whose country music it is.

—BILLY ALTMAN, *GQ,* 1996

Ricky Skaggs and George Strait can't do it all by theirselves.

—MEL TILLIS, on keeping traditional country music alive, 1988

It's all running together. It's all vanilla as far as I'm concerned.

—WAYLON JENNINGS, on the conformity of new country music, 1995

You turn on CMT [Country Music Television], and everybody looks the same and sounds the same. The music's become almost like wallpaper; the individuality seems to have disappeared.

—KEN LEVITAN, of Rising Tide, 1996

It seems like music is . . . about television. Used to be music was about music. Now, all you hear is a soundtrack of a video. The mood of the record used to carry the whole weight of the performance.

—MERLE HAGGARD, 1995

It just don't seem like it's the music that matters anymore. It seems like it's everything *but* the music that matters. A lot of people go out and buy tickets just because somebody looks good in a pair of Wranglers—they'll buy tickets just to see how he dances or see how he shakes his hips. Boy, that's hard to compete with.

—MARK CHESNUTT, 1995

In the 1960s and 1970s . . . it seemed like country [music] was ashamed of itself, like it was apologizing and wanted to be pop. But now it's the last bastion of song, with melodies and lack of artifice.

—PAM TILLIS, 1993

I'm a committed member of the country music community—artistically, soulfully, musicologically. And sometimes, as a human being, I've asked myself why doesn't country music return that to me?

—RODNEY CROWELL, 1994

I think country music has made it known that they're pretty much not interested in my music. I might as well go where I'm invited.

—EMMYLOU HARRIS, on moving toward adult alternative music, 1995

I KNEW I WAS BORN TO DO [COUNTRY MUSIC], AND I HIT THE GROUND RUNNIN'.

—MARTY STUART, 1995

It was inevitable. Everyone with my surname, like Jimmy and Roy and David, seemed to be into it.

—KENNY ROGERS, on getting into country music, 1993

The reason I got into this business in the first place was so I could drink whiskey, chase women, and have a good time. I could carry a tune and play the guitar, so it seemed like a good way to accomplish those things.

—TOM T. HALL, 1993

People would say, "You know, you should pursue [country music]. You're not that bad. . . . You're not that good, but you're not that bad!"

—JAMES BONAMY, 1996

I love country music. It's my home. I have never felt that it has slighted me. It was the format that held the ladder while I got to climb as high as I could. —GARTH BROOKS, 1994

I'm country, and that's the way I'm gonna stay. It's fed me real good. —LORETTA LYNN, 1978

I love country music, and it's my life. It's the only thing I ever cared for, and it's the only thing I ever will care for. I guess I care for it too much, more than the wives and personal things, but it's very important to me. And that's the way it is. —GEORGE JONES, 1988

Country music was like our [family's] religion. We were country music fans first, and then we were Baptists. —RONNIE DUNN, of Brooks & Dunn, 1996

I grew up on country. As a teenager, I listened to rock and pop, and I sang other music, but by the time I was about 20, I realized that it didn't touch me. It felt shallow for me to sing it. It didn't mean to me what country meant. Country felt like home. —MARTINA McBRIDE, 1996

I think of myself as a country artist. That, first and foremost. As long as I can have country hits, I don't care what happens. —CONWAY TWITTY (1933–1993)

Some people say I'm not real country. That's not true. Line up the Top 20 guys in cowboy hats and let's have a Webb Pierce sing-off and see who can sing the most Webb Pierce songs. I guarantee I'll win! I grew up on Merle Haggard and George Jones and I'm as country as cornbread. —COLLIN RAYE, 1996

People look at you, and they've got just the perfect little box for you, the perfect category. Call you redneck. Call you hillbilly. Like those were insults. —TRAVIS TRITT, 1994

A Hill-Billie is a free and untrammeled white citizen of Alabama, who lives in the hills, has no means to speak of, dresses as he can, talks as he pleases, drinks whiskey when he gets it, and fires off his revolver as the fancy takes him.

—*The New York Journal*, April 23, 1900

Call the band anything you want. We're nothing but a bunch of hillbillies from North Carolina and Virginia anyway.

—AL HOPKINS, whose band, the Hill Billies, [introduced] the term in connection with country and western music, 1925

In the old days, it was called "hillbilly music," but if you called somebody a hillbilly, you were making fun of him. Hillbilly meant inferior. I started telling record companies, "Let's not call it hillbilly; let's call it something else"—and I thought, why not call it "country"? The name stuck.

—ERNEST TUBB (1914–1984), who is credited with popularizing the term "country music"

> ## YOU GOT TO HAVE SMELT A LOT OF MULE MANURE TO SING LIKE A HILLBILLY.
> —HANK WILLIAMS (1923–1953)

What do you mean, "[It's] peasant music," you goddamned son of a bitch!

—FARON YOUNG, (1932–1996) to Zsa Zsa Gabor, 1988

Unfortunately . . . New York City, some of the bigger cities, are still convinced that country is a little bit backwards. I work doubly hard to show that we are pretty intelligent, and don't just sit on bales of hay.

—WYNONNA JUDD, 1996

Talk about a hen out of a coop! I really felt like one [when I played Carnegie Hall]. I'm telling you! But you know what? We made 'em show their true colors. We brought the country out of 'em if anybody did! They was sitting up there stomping their feet and yelling just like a bunch of hillbillies. Just like we do!

—PATSY CLINE (1932–1963)

If our audience has broadened, it's not because I've changed, but because people are listening and finding [we] don't have a hayseed hangin' out of [our] mouths. Also, people want the truth, and country music is that if it's nothing else.

—WAYLON JENNINGS, 1973

[Redneck] is a glorious absence of sophistication. And I think we're all guilty of it.   —JEFF FOXWORTHY, comic, 1996

[My] only exposure to country music was Saturday night, seven o'clock on *Hee Haw.* . . . Not exactly what I wanted to do for a living.

—JOHN BERRY, 1996

There's no doubt we'd never have gotten where we are today if we'd been stuck in the hootenanny craze. Country music's not down on the farm on a hay bale anymore, and boy, I'm damn glad of it.

—HANK WILLIAMS, JR., 1996

We get stereotyped, you know, the hay bales and settin' on the front porch. *The Beverly Hillbillies* and *Deliverance* are all that people know about Bluegrass music. We have all our teeth and all our hair. It's good music; people love it.

—LARRY STEPHENSON, bluegrass musician, 1996

This sounds like braggin', but you know, you can hear a lot of different groups on the stage, and bluegrass can go out there, and it's like the music just started there. It's got a music of its own, a hard-drivin' music, you see. It stands to itself.

—BILL MONROE (1911–1996), 1988

When other bands started playing [bluegrass], I think it was a threat to Bill Monroe, it came as a surprise to him. He felt that was imitation and competition, and it was only gradually that he realized he'd started a whole new style of music. It took him a long time to accept those other groups, the existence, as a compliment and a tribute, rather than a threat.

—JOHN W. RUMBLE, historian for the Country Music Foundation, 1996

You don't hear as much of the cheatin' thing. Country music is dealing with relationships now in a not-so-silly way.

—EDDIE RABBITT, 1993

[Music should be] a spontaneous, metamorphic tradition [with] covert sociopolitical overtones.

—DWIGHT YOAKAM, 1993

Sometimes we make ourselves artificially get away from our roots, but you don't have to. When something is based in a part of a person's soul, and indigenous to mankind and his hardships and his joys, when you get close to what mankind is all about and stay there, you can have fun with it, you can make a lot of people happy, and today you can make an awful lot of money doing it. I think [today's performers are] gonna see that the rudiments of simplicity will never be out of vogue.   —SAM PHILLIPS, founder of Sun Records, 1995

People fall in love with you for a sound or a song. And that goes for a certain spell. Then as an artist, you really have to dig inside your soul and try to figure out, without losin' what you've accomplished with your audience, how to stretch it on out, and keep cultivating your spiritual self, your musical self, your soul . . . whatever.

—MARTY STUART, 1996

There's a lot of people in this business that aren't good singers that have sure been big stars. I don't think that means anything in country music.   —HANK WILLIAMS, JR., 1988

I started playing music because it meant something to me, because it fulfilled me. The awards, all that, have never been the motivation. And they don't mean shit unless you're happy within yourself.

—MARY CHAPIN CARPENTER, 1993

In the face of the adversities, I still maintain that nothing matters but the music. You know, if I weren't getting paid, I'd probably still be fighting to do it.   —CLINT BLACK, 1993

I'm in music because it's what I am. I will always cut albums. I'll always sing, I'll always play. If it ever gets to be really big, then that's cool. If it just stays like it is, I've got enough.

—JOY LYNN WHITE, 1995

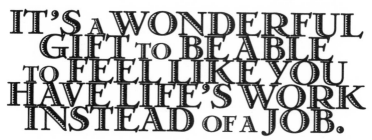

—KATHY MATTEA, 1996

I think of that Bob Dylan song: "Someday everything's gonna be different—when I paint my masterpiece." I want to paint a masterpiece before I leave this planet. To me, the sights on that masterpiece, with each passing day, just get higher and higher and higher. Almost something that I can't attain. But that'll keep me coming back to work tomorrow.   —RODNEY CROWELL, 1996

I think my albums are going to hold up well, but I don't think I've recorded my masterpiece. So that keeps me going, that pushes me, makes me stretch and grow as an artist and be the anxiety-ridden perfectionist that I am.   —PAM TILLIS, 1995

All you have at the end of the day when you go home and go to bed is the music—those 45 minutes on stage that you've been waiting your whole life for.   —ALISON KRAUSS, 1994

The music that I've chosen is music that does, in fact, span time. I can imagine "Through the Years," I can imagine "Lady," I can imagine

"The Gambler," I can imagine "Coward of the County" being played 20 years from now, representative of an era in music. That's what I was trying to do, was create a musical legacy that said, "Hey, I was here."

—KENNY ROGERS, 1996

Music saved my life. I'm just an emotional hurricane. If it wasn't for music, I would have been one screwed-up kid. It gave me focus, it gave me something to do, to put all my energy into.

—WYNONNA JUDD

Music will always be my first love and biggest kick.

—REBA McENTIRE, 1996

Music is not just my passion—it's my companion.

—RONNIE MILSAP

I THINK, SOMETIMES, THE MUSIC
JUST CHOOSES *YOU.*
—LEE ROY PARNELL, 1996

I'll tell you, here's the best way to describe my situation. Some people have their music. My music's got me.

—WAYLON JENNINGS, 1983

When I hear an artist sing a song, I can tell if they mean it. You can tell when someone's singing their brains out.

—WYNONNA JUDD, 1996

Don't play any music you don't believe in because it will definitely come back to haunt you.

—MARTY STUART, 1995

Sure, I want a radio hit, just like everybody else. But more than that, I want to be remembered. I want to be remembered as a man who didn't sell out. Look at Hank Williams! Look at Jimmie

Rodgers! . . . You work nine-to-five, you don't have a lot of money to buy records. You buy a record, you want a record that somebody's poured their heart and soul into. People can tell! People can tell! You can't fool people. . . . If I put out a record I didn't believe in, I'd be lying. And I won't do that.   —MARTY BROWN, 1993

[Patsy Cline] considered everything she recorded like an entry in her diary. "It's like writing a lot of personal things down on the page," she told me, "and wanting them just right so that when other people see it, they'll see how it was and how you really felt. Doing something I don't believe in makes me feel like a whore."
          —DONN HECHT, songwriter, 1993

This is what I do. In order to make [the music] work for me, and you, I have to be happy with it. I'll do whatever it takes to be happy with it, 'cause I *can't* be miserable doing the only thing I love to do.
          —SHELBY LYNNE, 1995

I would just like to see a little more consciousness in my music and in country music in general. Music is supposed to uplift, inform, move you. I don't want to end up being a smile that somebody remembers. I want to have said something to people.
          —LACY J. DALTON, 1993

I had a vision to make music, that music and my life could be used to bring something positive in this world.
          —BILLY RAY CYRUS, 1995

I want to [perform] for a good time, sure. But I want a lot more depth to go down than that. You can do that through the lyric content of your songs, through interviews, through the way you come off to the public. But I don't want us to be just the proverbial shit-howdy show out there on the road.
          —RONNIE DUNN, of Brooks & Dunn, 1994

I hate to say anything Mac Davis ever said, but I believe in music. It's one of the real hopes of the world.   —WAYLON JENNINGS, 1980

~13

I don't think every song has to have incredible content, intelligence, emotionally or socially. A lot of times people just want to hear music that makes 'em feel good. —ASHLEY CLEVELAND, 1996

Crowds come to see us and pay 10 to 20 dollars apiece to stand up and scream for two hours. It's probably very therapeutic. Psychiatrists encourage people to scream, holler, and laugh. Music raises their spirits, which is why they go to concerts. Music is a motivation. Music will make you leap off your ass and move.
—WILLIE NELSON, 1988

A good country song has one or more key ingredients: It feels good. You can relate to it. It pulls a heartstring or tickles a funnybone. It stirs an emotion or thought. You can move your body to it. Or tap your foot. Or clap your hands. —KENNY BEARD, songwriter, 1996

Music is a giving thing. It's a vehicle for me to share what I love about this life. —PHILLIP CLAYPOOL, 1996

Not everybody has the gift of writing, but they all do have the gift of feeling. And I think that's what's so wonderful about music—music speaks with the voice of the soul. —DOLLY PARTON, 1993

I brought a mandolin that I was considering on buying . . . over to [Bill Monroe] and I wanted to play it for him. I wanted him to listen and to see what he thought, you know, did it pass the Monroe test. He was playing it and he said, "Yeah, that's a good mandolin. You oughta buy that." We sat there and we played for an hour and we probably said 15 words. . . . I got up to leave and he said, "Boy, we talked about a lot of good things." Our spirits talked; we connected. That's what he loves to do. He'll talk, but he's a man of few words. His music has always spoken for him.
—RICKY SKAGGS, 1996

Music is all about communicating my true emotions out through the audience and back to me. —MARK O'CONNOR, fiddler, 1993

In a lot of ways I was a loner, but music has always been a bridge between me and people. Music is a vehicle into yourself and into other people and into the world around you and into the universe as well. And it's been a great friend to me.

—KOSTAS, songwriter, 1995

When you can see that what you're doin' is really movin' somebody, inside, where they live . . . it's a great feelin'! Nothin' hurts, nothin' matters, everything's great. That feelin' may not last but two or three minutes, every four or five months. But it's worth four or five months of tryin' to find it to feel it.   —DELBERT McCLINTON, 1996

What I do for a living is get people to feeling good.

—WILLIE NELSON, 1988

If you're out there on stage singing "What Might Have Been" and you got 40 people in the front row crying, you know you're doing something. To us, music is all about emotion.

—DUANE PROPES, of Little Texas, 1995

In country music we want wet eyes, not wet crotches.

—BOBBY BARE, 1984

COUNTRY MUSIC IS AMERICAN, IT STARTED HERE, IT'S OURS.

—RICHARD NIXON (1913–1995), 1974

Country music is our heritage. They oughta teach it in the schools.

—LOU STRINGER, publisher, 1970

As an important American phenomenon, [country music] deserves to be understood and taken seriously by all Americans. Unfortunately, country music has suffered from its humble beginnings away from the centers of power and influence, and from its sometimes embarrassing adherence to simple virtues which many find naive.

—DOROTHY HORSTMAN, *Sing Your Heart Out, Country Boy,* 1996

Ironically, it was after I moved to the West Coast that I turned around and wrote most acutely about my people, my family, my heritage. But that's not unusual when you think that sometimes you need to get out of the woods, get up on a clearing and look back, to know that you're not looking at tree bark, you're looking at a forest. And the perspective I have is because I moved away.

—DWIGHT YOAKAM, 1996

TWANG IS WHAT YOU FEEL THE EMOTION FROM IN COUNTRY MUSIC. AS "SOUL" IS TO RHYTHM AND BLUES, "TWANG" IS TO COUNTRY.

—JANIS CARNES, 1993

Country music is white blues. I mean, to me, Ray Charles is the father of [modern] black blues, and George Jones is the country singer of the white blues. It's that sound. They're completely different, but they strike the same kind of chord, to me.

—EMMYLOU HARRIS, 1988

We used to say that country music was the white man's blues, and blues, of course, was the black man's blues.　　　—B. B. KING, 1996

Country music and blues are close, close relatives. It's the same man singin' the same song about the good and the bad times, a woman he's got, a woman he wants, and one he can't get rid of.

—WAYLON JENNINGS, 1996

Country music speaks emotional truth. Rock has drifted away from it. Country is soul music for white people, and people always return to soul music, because that's where the feeling is.

—PAUL SHAFFER, musician and David Letterman's bandleader, 1994

Unlike rock 'n' roll, and unlike classical, there is something about country music that touches the heart of the common man.

—RICKY SKAGGS, 1996

It's not the instrument or the arrangement that makes country music, it's the soul and the performance. Otherwise, Dean Martin could be the biggest country singer in the world.

—WAYLON JENNINGS, 1973

There's a lot of debate about country music. What is country music. But I know that I'm from the country, and for me, that makes anything I do country. —STEVE RIPLEY, of the Tractors, 1996

I don't know what country is. I haven't figured it out yet. Everybody who complains, "Let's keep country country," well, what the hell *is* country? Once you pass Roy Acuff and Bill Monroe, you've passed country. I think every artist has his own particular type of music. I do Marty Robbins–type music. If you want to call it country, that's fine. —MARTY ROBBINS (1925–1982)

Country music is whatever country people buy.

—KENNY ROGERS, 1996

Hell, I know what I'm doing, all right. I'm just playing the kind of music my kind of folks like to hear.

—BOB WILLS (1905–1975)

True country music is honesty, sincerity, and real life to the hilt.

—GARTH BROOKS

Country music is simply three chords and the truth.

—HAL KETCHUM, 1996

COUNTRY MUSIC IS THE MUSIC THAT LOOKS AT REAL LIFE WITH AN HONEST EYE.

—BILL IVEY, executive director of the Country Music Foundation, 1996

I thought country music was just a bunch of people hangin' on to their noses and singing! —ANNE MURRAY

I was raised in the country and can remember taking a bath in the kitchen with the radio on top of the ice box playing country music. Most of us have, somewhere in our background, the sound of a banjo being plucked or a fiddle being played. But we're not satisfied with three chords and bass and a steel [guitar]. That's our heritage, but we want to offer a whole lot more.

—JOHN D. LOUDERMILK, songwriter, 1970

I don't like to be categorized. I don't like to be corralled or fenced in. I think there's only two categories for songs: good and bad. And whether it's pop, contemporary, traditional, whatever it is, once I sing it, it's gonna be country. —REBA McENTIRE, 1995

I suppose categories serve a purpose, but the [country music] boundaries are definitely bleeding, and that's good. I think it's an obvious thing to do, to bring [musical] worlds together. The collaborative aspect of music drives it forward.

—EMMYLOU HARRIS, 1995

There are different levels of country music. When you go to a restaurant you don't order the same thing every time. Cole Porter says "I love you" one way, Hank Williams says it another way. It's a matter of how much salt you put on your eggs.

—OWEN BRADLEY, producer, 1970

If everybody did the same kind of song, you wouldn't need but one guy singin'.   —MEL TILLIS, 1988

You imitate the people you love till you come up with your own style.

—PAM TILLIS, 1996

I think sometimes, as artists, we will become good at something and get our little formula together, how we create, and then destroy it. You know, and then put it back together again. [Then], hopefully, there's a new dimension or a new element that makes us unique.   —RODNEY CROWELL, 1996

I guess there's a transformation taking place, or something. I don't really know how to explain it. But once I get the guitar on and start doing that thing, there's no problem.

—CONWAY TWITTY (1933–1993), on overcoming his shyness

Bar fights are tough on guitars. They fall down, the neck cracks. There goes your old favorite. Harder on acoustic guitars than an old Stratocaster. You could probably chop wood with a Strat.

—TRAVIS TRITT, 1994

Beyond making a living with a guitar, the guitar makes you happy. To me it was designed for happiness, sorrow, and emotion. There's something about when you're lonely and you pick up a guitar and make yourself grin. All the loneliness disappears. It's a good way to meet girls. I can't think of anything that a guitar can do wrong.

—MARTY STUART, 1994

When I'm learning a song, part of it's just sitting down with a guitar and finding the key and then finding where I belong in it; how I fit in with that song. If I could explain it better I would, but I think it's something that you just sort of throw yourself into. It's like riding a wave. You don't really know where you're gonna end up.

—EMMYLOU HARRIS, 1996

There are things I want to play [on the banjo] that I haven't been able to yet. Like improvising. That can be a very spiritual experience. Stuff you don't even know pours out. I want to become more tuned in to pulling off the notes I hear in my head at the exact moment I hear them. It's a lifelong goal.　　—BELA FLECK, 1994

I believe every guitar has a certain amount of songs in it. Once you write 'em out of it, you got to put it away.

—LEE ROY PARNELL, 1996

I CAN READ MUSIC, BUT NOT ENOUGH
TO HURT MY PICKIN', MAN.
—GLEN CAMPBELL, 1970

I'm the Danny Partridge of country music because I pretend to play [the bass] and make a living at it.

—ROBERT REYNOLDS, of the Mavericks, 1996

I heard a guy say one time, that if you took out Bill Monroe's brain, it would be in the shape of an F-5 mandolin.

—RICKY SKAGGS, 1996

We get asked this question all the time, "What makes y'all's sound?" And I really honest and truly don't think that any of us actually know. I hope we never figure it out 'cause we might change it.

—MARTY RAYBON, of Shenandoah, 1996

[Baseball] gave me a feel for team sports, and that's probably how I got to playing music in a band. I always loved the camaraderie of playing off each other in team atmosphere. You know, you got your pitchers and your lead singers, and you got your catchers [and your] drummer.　　—LARRY STEWART, 1996

I really believe that simplicity don't need to be greased.

—BILLY JOE SHAVER, on keeping the music simple, 1993

Less is more. It doesn't take a lot of fancy [guitar] licks and a lot of fancy lyrics to get to people.

—JEFF HANNA, of the Nitty Gritty Dirt Band, 1996

My deal is, if you can't hear the guy next to you, then you're playing [guitar] too loud, or he ain't playin' loud enough.

—LEE ROY PARNELL, 1994

We tend to equate excitement in music with how hard a drum is hit.

—EMMYLOU HARRIS, 1996

Instruments don't make country. We're entitled to a heavy rock beat if it complements our songs. Or if we want to use a kazoo played through a sewer pipe, all right too.

—WAYLON JENNINGS, 1985

When I sing, to me, every word has a feeling about it. I had to linger, had to hold it. . . . I didn't want to let go of that no more than I wanted to let go of the woman I loved.

—LEFTY FRIZZELL (1928–1975), on his distinctive note-bending style

A guitar pulling is where songwriters gather in somebody's room and fight it out for attention and approval. You might say it's like a bunch of Old West gunfighters coming together to see who is best—only instead of slapping their holsters and coming up with six-guns blazing, they unsnap their guitar cases and come up singing.

—WILLIE NELSON, 1988

WRITING THE SONGS

An old songwriter named Frank Dycus told me once that if you've got to explain the damn [song], you've got no business singing it to start with. —TRAVIS TRITT, 1994

I'm not comfortable with songs that provide answers. I like songs that just deal with the questions. —EMMYLOU HARRIS, 1995

A good country song takes a page out of somebody's life and puts it to music. —CONWAY TWITTY (1933–1993)

I TAKE A WHOLE LIFE STORY AND COMPRESS IT INTO THREE MINUTES.
—HARLAN HOWARD

A song ain't nothin' in the world but a story just wrote with music to it. —HANK WILLIAMS (1923–1953)

I'm basically a storyteller. I draw some kind of conclusion from living X-amount of years and try to put that into song form . . . so I can remember. —MAC McANALLY, songwriter, 1996

I write songs that might illustrate a point, might give you this or that, but basically, they're stories. And a story can express a viewpoint much better than a lecture. —DAVID MASSENGILL, singer-songwriter, 1996

You sing about the things [people] think about most, but don't talk about. That becomes an emotional outlet for the people, and they feel they have a friend in the song. They like it, buy it, they play it, they sing it, because it's something that seems to fit their purpose.

—WEBB PIERCE, 1996

It's so strange, you'll be playing and you'll look out and you'll key on a few different people. . . . When you see them mouthing the words to a song you've written, it's really a neat feeling. There's something universal going on there that says, "Yeah! That's what it's all about." —DUNCAN CAMERON, of Sawyer Brown, 1996

I have people constantly asking me, "How can you show yourself like this? Don't you feel self-conscious about it?" And I say, "I just feel like it's necessary." I want to make people think, and make a statement. Otherwise, what's the point?

—LUCINDA WILLIAMS, on revealing herself in her songs

Just because I make records and write songs, I don't want to throw my private life open for inspection. Yet I use songwriting in a real self-indulgent way, as therapy. And once I sing it, I have to live with it.

—ROSANNE CASH

I drop myself into a place of role-playing when I write, or that's what I think I'm doing. Maybe that's why psychologists or psychiatrists use role-playing as a means to address the self. Because what you do is you think you've disguised yourself from reality for the purposes of articulation, and in reality you've probably exposed yourself. —DWIGHT YOAKAM, 1996

> YOU HAVE TO FILL THAT NOTHING;
> IT CALLS ON YOU. IT'S THE
> GREAT VOID.
> —JO CAROL PIERCE, on the drive to write songs, 1994

You [write songs] because you love it, it makes you feel good. You have to do it; you have no choice. —JOIE SCOTT, songwriter, 1996

When I started, I wrote about hate and bitterness. Eventually, I threw those songs away, but the experience was better than a psychiatrist and a whole lot cheaper. —JAN HOWARD, 1994

The sad part about happy endings is there's nothing to write about. —TAMMY WYNETTE, 1993

There's this fear that if you take the drugs away and you take some of the risk taking away, that you won't write anymore. —STEVE EARLE, on getting straight and sober, 1996

Sometimes, I joke that I'm gonna go out and get married and divorced so I can come up with the next album. —TRAVIS TRITT, 1993

I tend to average about 10 hit songs per ex-wife. —VERN GOSDIN

There's only about five things, six at the most, to say about a man and a woman and this thing called love. But yet, within that, it's still refreshing how original writers can be with those five or six stories. —HARLAN HOWARD, 1994

[Harlan Howard] told me the most important revelation he ever had was that it had all been said before, and that it's more about saying something from your own perspective and being true to your own feelings instead of struggling to be unique. And I've really found that to be the truth. —HAL KETCHUM, 1996

Songs are like jokes: there's not an original one anywhere. —ARCHIE CAMPBELL

I found out a lot of that shit I learned in school about writing doesn't apply. —MEL TILLIS, 1995

~25

When you write from experience like I do, relationships are some of the greatest things that can happen to you as far as creating material. It's a great thing, I guess, to be able to take something that's so devastatingly bad and pull some good out of it.   —TRAVIS TRITT, 1995

I'd say that 99 percent of what I write has come from my own experience. A person could probably start from my first song and go all the way to my last—if he knew what to look for—and write my autobiography.   —WILLIE NELSON, 1980

Songwriting, or writing generally, is not something that you literally have to live. For a long time I didn't write because I felt like, if I didn't literally live an experience, well, I can't write about it, or you can't take any poetic literary liberty to create. But that's what creative writing is. And ultimately, you are creating, maybe only unconsciously, the inner self.   —DWIGHT YOAKAM, 1996

If you ain't lived it, there ain't no use in singin' it.

—SAMMY KERSHAW

You don't have to live it, but you do have to feel it.

—ALLEN FRIZZELL, repeating his brother Lefty Frizzell's songwriting advice, 1996

Write from the heart, not the head.   —MARK MILLER, of Sawyer Brown

Each song doesn't have to be autobiographical. I'm a pretty good listener for my friends. I like people to tell me what's going on with their lives. So later I can turn it against them in a song.

—KIM RICHEY, songwriter, 1996

I like meaty subjects. I think the struggles that people go through just in the course of living are really fascinating. The way people deal with [those struggles]. That's what really engages me as a writer.

—GRETCHEN PETERS, 1996

This life is a hard row to hoe, and "hard-row-to-hoe" songs are going to be the most popular.   —TED HARRIS, songwriter, 1996

I have different [songs] I love as a singer and as a writer. It's like having a houseful of kids. You're partial to all of them.

—DOLLY PARTON, 1993

I think the writers of today maybe put emphasis in a little different place or two than we did. I think the melodies in songs are more important. We used to use the melody as something to hum while the words were goin' by.

—BILL ANDERSON, 1995

If you're writing about a building, you make it a big, tall one so you've got as much to write about as you possibly can.

—CLINT BLACK, 1995

You can't try to write a big-sounding song, because if you do, it'll end up pretentious. What you do is try to write about the little things in life, and sometimes that unlocks a real big emotion.

—JAMES HOUSE, singer-songwriter, 1996

I never wanted to be an elitist and be too intellectual. So truck drivers can understand what I'm saying.

—LUCINDA WILLIAMS

It's so important to me to make sure the average person can understand what I'm trying to say. Songwriting at its best is very rarely poetry; it's usually narrative and practically journalism. It's a form of literature, but one you can consume while you're driving your car.

—STEVE EARLE

Make your melodies simple enough so that the average person can hum them.

—TOM T. HALL

PART OF LEARNING WHAT TO WRITE IS LEARNING WHAT TO LEAVE OUT.

—GUY CLARK

I think you can fix a good song right into being a bad song if you work it too hard in the studio. —TRACY BYRD, 1996

Ernest Tubb [said] the two most important things for a singer are clarity of thought and individual style. He said there are thousands of people who can sing on the beat but not many with a clarity of message. If you don't say your words plain, like Ernest always did . . . then you damn sure can't sell them a song.

—WILLIE NELSON, 1988

Ideas are a dime a dozen. I could sit here for 10 minutes and come up with 10 good ideas for a song. The idea comes from the mind, but the song comes from the heart. —HANK MILLS, songwriter, 1970

I JUST SIT DOWN FOR A FEW MINUTES, DO A LITTLE THINKING, AND GOD WRITES THE SONGS FOR ME.
—HANK WILLIAMS (1923–1953)

The song just came, arrived, like it had been there all along, waiting for me to find it. —TRAVIS TRITT, on writing his first song, 1994

You see, I go through periods where I really feel like I have this identity, I feel like I know who I am: I'm a songwriter . . . I'm something. And then, when I'm not writing songs, it's like I've lost my identity and I've gotta get it back again.

—MARY CHAPIN CARPENTER, 1995

Music is my form of expression. . . . It's mine. It's the only thing I've had all my life that's mine. —LYNN LANGHAM, songwriter, 1996

I don't have real good words sometimes to express how I feel. And even if I do have the words, I'm not that comfortable. We, as "macho guys," sometimes don't have it in us, and don't feel very good about expressing . . . how we feel . . . for people we love. Did I say that right?

LARRY STEWART, on letting his songs do the talking, 1996

I could no more not write than not breathe.

—KRIS KRISTOFFERSON

If I go a day without writing, it's like a smoker going a day without a cigarette.　　　　　　　　　　　　　　　—NANCI GRIFFITH

When I write a song, I have to be alone. I'm another person. I live [as] this person until I have the song written. If it's a honky-tonk girl, I put myself into becoming a honky-tonk girl. If anybody walked into that room when I was writin', they may not even recognize me, 'cause I take on another look.　　　—LORETTA LYNN, 1988

I wrap my head in aluminum foil and sit on top of a mobile home.

—BOBBIE CRYNER, on where she gets her musical inspiration, 1996

The guy who plays accordion for me called me from Austin last week. I'd left an envelope in his car with the lyrics to a song . . . that I'd written in its entirety on the bus one day before sound check at a show and forgotten completely about. Fortunately, that's the way I write: anywhere, anytime. I'm open 24 hours a day.

—HAL KETCHUM, 1996

Songwriting is like life: long periods of struggle with intermittent moment of satisfaction.　　　　　　　　—MIKE REID, songwriter, 1996

A lot of songs you write are just for exercise—just pencil sharpeners.

—HARLAN HOWARD

When I get to writing, it will come in spurts. Then . . . I figure that's the last song I'll ever write, because I just run the barrel dry. Then I go into a slump where I don't write anything. That's why I like to hang out with other writers—you inspire each other.

—WAYLON JENNINGS, 1984

When you get in a slump, you feel so bad you wonder who did write those songs, the ones with your name on them. You lose your confidence. I've done that, but I've always fought my way back. I've just really bore down, and even if I have to write a few terrible songs, I eventually work my way back up to the mark.

—HARLAN HOWARD, 1994

There is nothing more intimidating than a blank sheet of paper.

—VICTORIA SHAW, songwriter, 1995

I would like to write more songs. And I feel that there's a certain lazy streak and reticent streak in me to put the time and effort into it. The fear is of writing a mediocre song, not just a bad song. In fact, I'd almost rather write a bad song.

—EMMYLOU HARRIS, 1996

I need time off to get input, or else nothing'll come out.

—CLINT BLACK, 1996

I'm not a very productive writer. Something has to hit me really strong, due to the fact I'm lazy.   —WAYLON JENNINGS, 1994

I started writing music because I got tired of looking in the bottom drawer for material after everyone else had turned it down. It was like picking out your cleanest dirty shirt.   —VERN GOSDIN, 1994

I heard Marty [Stuart] blister that mandolin, and I gave up the mandolin. Then I heard [Ricky Skaggs] play the fiddle, and I gave up the fiddle, too. . . . That's [when] I became a songwriter.

—MARK COLLIE, 1996

I'm a writer trying to get out of a singer's body.

—TANYA TUCKER, 1996

I'm an interpreter. I like to take another man's song and make it sound like I wrote it. I'm a fan of writers.

—WAYLON JENNINGS, 1985

I was a musician but I wanted to write. I was unlike any other in Nashville. Patsy [Cline] thought my music was unique and wonderful. Of course, I agreed with her. That made *two* of us.

—ROGER MILLER (1936–1992)

If there is one thing I have known I am good at since I was old enough to catch the first thoughts and sounds that passed through me, it is songwriting. —WILLIE NELSON, 1988

I've come to the viewpoint that lean dogs run a long time, and it's best to stay hungry, on top of things, creative and fresh, rather than nail something out to stay fat and happy. —RADNEY FOSTER, 1995

This ain't no magic show. It's about the song and the music, and the song is the star. —JIM ROONEY, Hal Ketchum's producer, 1995

—CONWAY TWITTY (1933–1993)

Mama songs are always good for country music.

—JOHNNY CASH, 1996

I'm going to go home and call you back and play a tune called "Detroit City." So when you answer, if nobody talks, don't hang up, 'cause it's me.

—MEL TILLIS, aka the Stutterin' Boy, pitching a song to Jimmy Dean, 1989

I didn't like "Stand by Your Man." I had no faith in that song at all. I think I should record another that I don't like, and maybe that would do it. —TAMMY WYNETTE, on having another hit single, 1988

["Coat of Many Colors"] is a true story, and means more to me than any other song I've ever recorded. There were 12 children in our family, and we were real poor. . . . As far as money to buy clothes, all we had was what Mama made. I was about eight years old, and it was my first year in a big public school. . . . Somebody had sent her a box of scraps to make quilts out of, and she took them and made me a little coat out of it. . . . It hurt me so bad when the kids laughed, because I was so proud of it. I especially liked the bright colors, and I thought I was the prettiest thing in school.   —DOLLY PARTON, 1996

"Ruby, Don't Take Your Love to Town," is based on a true story of a man [who] was injured during World War II in Germany and was sent to England to recuperate. While he was in England, he met a nurse that helped nurse him back to health. He married her and brought her back home. . . . His wounds kept recurring, and he'd have to go to the veterans' hospital and became temporarily paralyzed. . . . "Ruby" stood by him till she could stand it no longer. Then she started fixing her hair, putting flowers in it, painting her lips, and walking back and forth in front of the pool room. She was lonesome, needed attention. . . . I just changed the wars and brought it up to date and wrote the story in about an hour. Eventually, it was a couple of years ago, he killed her and himself too. That's a true story.   —MEL TILLIS, 1996

After being barraged by Women's Lib and ERA, I wanted ["Stand by Your Man"] to be a song for all the women out there who didn't agree, a song for the truly liberated woman, one who is secure enough in her identity to enjoy it. Even though to some skeptics it may hint of chauvinism, as far as I'm concerned, they can like it or lump it. Because [the song] is just another way of saying "I love you"—without reservations.   —BILLY SHERRILL, 1996

It took me six weeks to write "King of the Road." I was driving from Davenport, Iowa, to Chicago, and somewhere along the way I saw a sign on the road which read, "Trailers for Sale or Rent," and for some reason that phrase stuck in my mind. It wasn't until later, in Boise, Idaho, that I really sat down and made something out of it . . . although I had to induce labor to get it completed. I got stuck after the first verse, so I went out to a Boise store and bought a statuette of a hobo. I sat and stared at it until the rest of the tune came to me. —ROGER MILLER (1936–1992)

I had just gone to work for Combine Music. Fred Foster, the owner, called me and said, "I've got a title for you: 'Me and Bobbie McKee,' " . . . I thought he said, "McGee." . . . I thought there was no way I could ever write that, and it took me months hiding from him, because I can't write on assignment. But it must have stuck in the back of my head. One day I was driving between Morgan City and New Orleans. It was raining and the windshield wipers were going. . . . I took an old experience with another girl in another country. I had it finished by the time I got to Nashville.
—KRIS KRISTOFFERSON, 1996

Years ago I was playing a one-nighter near San Francisco. I happened to overhear a couple arguing at the corner table right next to the bandstand. I heard the woman say, "If you'd release me, we wouldn't have any problems and everything would be all right." It didn't hit me then, but it did later, just thinking about them arguing. . . . I had always felt that divorce was a dirty word in a song, and I felt that "Release Me" was a softer way of saying it. The song has sold over 18 million records and has been recorded over 300 times. —EDDIE MILLER, songwriter, 1996

Me and Willie [Nelson] wrote ["Good Hearted Woman"] while playing poker with two guys. We wrote the whole song during that game and didn't miss a hand. We danced every set and lost our ass but we wrote ourselves a pretty good song.
—WAYLON JENNINGS, 1996

["My Mary"] was written about my first real sweetheart. When I left Texas and came out to California, all I could ever do was to dream of the Texas beauty that I'd left behind. I couldn't see then how I could ever go on through life without her. . . . She married an old friend of mine. I never saw Mary again, nor her husband, for about 25 years, but one time they came out to California and looked me up. Mary had sure put on the weight. She . . . tipped the scales at, at least two hundred pounds, and had acquired a very bossy attitude towards men. . . . There's a verse of scripture in the Bible that reads, "The Lord giveth and the Lord taketh away." The Lord giveth her to me, but, thank God, he taketh her away and gave her to my friend. Through all my life God has been so good to me.

—STUART HAMBLEN, singer-songwriter, 1996

Lefty [Frizzell] said, "Why don't you stay and write a song with us?" And I said, "Lefty, I been up for over two days and a night. I've been [drinkin'], and I'm sobered up now, and my head's hurtin', and I don't feel good, and I just can't think. . . . That's the way life goes." Lefty said, "No, that's the way love goes." And he says, "Can I have that for an idea?" And I said, "You sure can." He said, "Well, why don't you stay and write it with us?" And I didn't do it.

—DOODLE OWENS, on passing up the opportunity to cowrite the hit song, "That's the Way Love Goes," 1996

At the time Hank wrote ["I Saw the Light"], he and his band had ended a tour and were getting near Montgomery, Alabama, in a car that didn't run too well. They were afraid they wouldn't make it. Then Hank spotted the beacon light at the Montgomery airport and said, "We're gonna make it now; I saw the light."

—AUDREY WILLIAMS, Hank Williams's wife, 1996

I had a brother-in-law that was always knocking his wife around and drank a lot. I got to thinking that maybe one day she'd just have enough and leave, so I wrote a song called "Too Late." I recorded it as my first number on Decca and it was a smash. I went to Oklahoma City and I ran into my brother-in-law. And he said, "Man, you never wrote anything as pretty as 'Too Late' in your life." I said, "You should like it, you son of a bitch, it's the story of your life."

—JIMMY WAKELY, songwriter, 1996

["We Could"] was a birthday present to my husband, Boudleaux. We were working in the basement house. He was laying on the couch; he likes to lay on the couch when he's working [on a song]. I was sitting in the chair directly across from him and he fell asleep.

I kept looking at him and thinking, "How precious," and I thought, "If anybody could make this old world whistle, we could, we could." If you want to talk about inspirational tunes, that song came so fast it was all I could do to write it down.

—FELICE BRYANT, 1996

I sold out a little bit on ["Tobacco Road"], I'm sorry to say, because I said, "Mother died and Daddy got drunk," but Mother didn't die at childbirth, and I never saw my dad take a drink in his life. Never heard him say a cussword, either. He was a marvelous man. At the time, I was just starting out in the music business, and I was frankly hungry.

—JOHN D. LOUDERMILK, 1996

I was really proud of ["Nobody Wins"]. It was kind of like I thought of myself as a songwriter finally. I remember I stopped putting "bartender" on my [tax forms] after that 'cause I'd made some money.

—KIM RICHEY, songwriter, 1996

Nobody laughs outrageously loud and makes a scene and falls over [in Nashville]. Everyone is very, very well behaved. I always refer to them as housebroken Texans.

—K. T. OSLIN, on the difference between Nashville and New York, 1993

I hope you all like what we do. If you don't, don't ever come down to Nashville. We'll kick the hell out of you.

—WAYLON JENNINGS, to a New York audience, 1973

Nashville doesn't like western songs at all. They're trying to sell country music to the Yankees and they want it all watered down, not too outrageous for the Yankees to stomach.   —ALVIN CROW

L.A. is a musician's town. New York is a lawyer's town. Nashville is a songwriter's town.   —BOB McDILL

Nashville cats, man. They play stuff in their sleep other dudes can't match in a month.   —PATRICK CARR, journalist, 1993

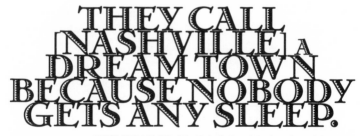

THEY CALL [NASHVILLE] A DREAM TOWN BECAUSE NOBODY GETS ANY SLEEP.

—PAUL HEMPHILL, *The Nashville Sound: Bright Lights and Country Music*

These guys [in my band] ain't moody. They're not weird, they're not on drugs, there's no problems. Everybody's just good ole country boys havin' a great time. I mean, I've hired guys out of Nashville or somewhere else, but they were too damned serious, always crying about stuff. —MARK CHESNUTT, 1995

I'd get nervous. I just didn't feel comfortable in that kinda situation. You'd walk into the studio and they'd put six guys behind you who'd never seen your music before, and it's impossible to get the feel of it in a three-hour session. —WILLIE NELSON, on recording in Nashville, 1985

They wouldn't let me pick my own songs. They wouldn't let me use my own band in the studio. . . . I'd cut a basic track, and by the time they were through adding stuff, I didn't even recognize it anymore. They also complained about the way I dressed, and that my hair was too long, though it was pretty short in those days.

—WAYLON JENNINGS, on his treatment in Nashville, 1984

I got so fuckin' sick of hearin' people say, "Oh, God. Your poor ole daddy, he wasn't treated right. He was the King and we loved him." Well, they *hated* Daddy in Nashville.

—HANK WILLIAMS, JR., 1988

I like Nashville an awful lot. I just wonder sometimes if Nashville likes me. —STEVE EARLE

It's like what Steve Earle said [about Nashville]. . . . It's definitely a relationship I don't want to disintegrate. At the same time . . . I'm not going to prostitute myself to make amends with a group of people who I didn't do anything to offend in the first place.

—TRAVIS TRITT, 1994

I think Nashville really is a town of creative musicians and song-writers. Without them, it would just be another Branson or Las Vegas, another glitzy, hollow entertainment resort.

—MARK O'CONNOR, 1993

The trouble is, they don't want writers like me in Nashville. They want sensitive types. They want a rock sound down there now, which they pass off as country music. My stuff isn't what they want to hear. —DALE WATSON, songwriter-performer, 1995

The problem came from right here in Nashville. They control it, they're the roots of it. And they call this "Music City, U.S.A., the Home of Country Music." They should be ashamed.

—GEORGE JONES, on the pop direction much of country music has taken, 1995

One of the last American myths is being cut off: that you could get off a Greyhound bus with your life savings of $40, your acoustic guitar wrapped in duct tape, and go into Nashville and write those songs, and you would . . . hang out on Lower Broad and get into Tootsie's. Well, you can't get into Tootsie's anymore without a booking agent. The people that have cleaned that up—the mayor and the chamber of commerce—are taking away Nashville's myth. And they don't know what they're going to miss until it's gone.

—DAN BAIRD, 1996

I can't tell you how many times I end up frustrated after turning on my country music radio station and hearing five or six newcomers, who all sound like either Joe Diffie, Clint Black, or Garth Brooks. Nashville has this cookie-cutter approach and the fans suffer.

—TRAVIS TRITT, 1995

If you look at the entire picture of Nashville currently, there's a lot of schlock that won't be here two years from now that people will have made a lot of money off of. That's the idea of big business.

—MARTY STUART, 1995

It's the record-making machine that I hate. That's my big gripe about Nashville. And that machine is a money eater, it's a glutton for money, and if you don't have the big bucks behind you, you don't get nowhere. —JOHNNY CASH, 1994

> # I'M NOT LEAVING COUNTRY. I'M JUST
> # TAKIN' IT WITH ME.
> —DOLLY PARTON, on her move from Nashville managers to an L.A. team, 1977

I hear all kinds of rumors out of Nashville that Johnny Cash is trying to go rock 'n' roll. I'm the first one to know that I'm too old to rock 'n' roll.   —JOHNNY CASH, 1994

THE GRAND OLE OPRY

Nashville is and always has been the spiritual home of country music, "hillbilly heaven," a fact properly noted in more than one country song . . . and it is never so evident as on a warm weekend, when the crowds pour into town for the Friday- and Saturday-night Opry performances—coming in from an average of 500 miles away by every means imaginable, living out of campers in downtown parking lots, strolling up and down Opry Place and Broadway in their Western clothes . . . having a beer at Tootsie's Orchid Lounge, taking one of the tour buses from the Opry House so they can see Music Row and Hank Williams' old home . . . and finally squatting on the curb in front of the ugly red-brick Grand Ole Opry House three hours before the doors open, sitting there emptying a box of Minnie Pearl's Fried Chicken and trying to figure out a way to get in for a show that was sold out seven weeks in advance.

—PAUL HEMPHILL, *The Nashville Sound: Bright Lights and Country Music*

The Ryman [Auditorium] wasn't air-conditioned and, especially in the summer, most of us couldn't get out the back door and across the alley into Tootsie's second-floor room fast enough—Patsy [Cline], Charlie [Dick], Bill [West], me and the clique. . . . [Tootsie's] was nothing more than a roadhouse, but it was like a second home. The tables had red-and-white checkered tablecloths and tin ashtrays and napkin holders. The walls were covered with hundreds and hundreds of autographs. We loved to go there, if for no other reason than to have Maggie's hamburgers and chili.

—DOTTIE WEST (1932–1991)

I recorded a song called "I Fall to Pieces," and I was in a car wreck. Now I'm really worried, because I have a brand-new record, and it's called "Crazy."
—PATSY CLINE (1932–1963), to her Opry audience

I'D LIKE TO SING YOU OLD FARTS A SONG!

—MARTY STUART, upon being inducted into the Grand Ole Opry, 1992

There's a piece of floor that was brought from the Ryman Auditorium that they integrated into the regular hardwood floor onstage. Every time I go out there and stand on that piece of wood, [I] can't help but think, "Roy Acuff stood here." I never walk onstage at the Opry that I don't feel humbled by bein' there. It's a special feelin'.
—CHARLIE DANIELS, 1996

[Playing the Opry] is one of the few performances in this world that will make my knees shake a little bit.
—TRAVIS TRITT, 1996

The first time I played on the Opry stage, I met Roy Acuff that night. He asked me, "Were your knees shakin'? Were you scared to death? Were you shakin' in your boots?" I said, "Yessir, I was." He said, "Good. When you lose that, I ain't got nothin' for you."
—MARK CHESNUTT, 1996

You didn't get on the Opry back [in the early days] for singing a song or having a hit number. They didn't ask you if you ever recorded. They didn't care. You had to be a showman. The only way you could get on was to have something to show and prove it. [My first night] . . . I did the "Great Speckled Bird," and . . . the audience stood and cheered and cheered. I tried to leave but they brought me back two, three times.
—ROY ACUFF (1903–1992)

There's been a lot of people who've sold records, but if you ain't played the Opry, you ain't done jack.

—HENRY PAUL, of Blackhawk, after playing the Opry for the first time, 1996

When you've been thrown out of Nero's Cactus Canyon Steak House—and I have been—how are you ever gonna get on the Grand Ole Opry? —KRIS KRISTOFFERSON, 1977

The band kicked off a song, and I tried to take the microphone off the stand. In my nervous frenzy, I couldn't get it off. That was enough to make me explode in a fit of anger. I took the mike stand, threw it down, then dragged it along the edge of the stage. There were 52 lights, and I wanted to break all 52, which I did.

—JOHNNY CASH, on the night he was asked not to return to the Grand Ole Opry, 1993

When Bob Wills went on the Grand Ole Opry he was already a huge star in Texas but not so much in Nashville. . . . Bob went onstage with his cigar in his mouth. They told him not to smoke on the stage, and he walked off again. So far as I know, that was his one and only appearance on the Opry. —WILLIE NELSON, 1988

I PLAYED THE GRAND OLE OPRY TWICE.
BUT THE SECOND TIME I BROUGHT A
JAZZ BAND IN AND THEY NEVER
ASKED ME BACK.
—JONI MITCHELL, 1996

Judge Hay [the Opry founder] would be turning over in his grave if he were here now, seeing men dressing the way they are and hearing the kind of music they're doing. Every Saturday night, just before it was time for the Opry to start, he'd go backstage and say, "Let's keep it close to the ground, boys."

—GRANT TURNER, veteran Opry announcer, 1970

I won't pretend that I wanted to be on *The Grand Ole Opry* because I had been a fan all my life. I had never thought about it one way or the other, except that I didn't particularly like the music. I had never even gone to see an Opry broadcast, much less felt a desire to be on the show.   —MINNIE PEARL (1912–1996), 1993

It used to be that the old girl would say to her old man, "Let's go to the Opry," and he'd go reluctantly, because all he was going to get to listen to was old hairy-legged Ray Price, Roy Acuff, Marty Robbins, and so on. But when it got to where these boy fans could hear Kitty [Wells] sing a love ballad, why naturally, they were a lot more eager to go.

—DEE KILPATRICK, Opry manager, 1993

I think the Opry is fast coming into equality.

—JEAN SHEPARD, on women in the Grand Ole Opry, 1996

We are a pretty close bunch, and have shared a lot of love, hurt, pain, good times and bad, and a lot of colds and coughs. We've enjoyed each other's loves, husbands, children, and grandchildren, hit records, flops, misfortunes, and fortunes. We've borrowed belts, buckles, shoes, jewelry, makeup, mirrors, underslips, hair spray, perfume, and shoes from each other. We've watched each other grow up, grow older. . . . People think the girl singers fight and pull each other's hair, and that's not true at all. I still love my Opry sisters.

—JEANNE PRUETT, 1993

Different [Opry] girls started calling and saying I ought to return to the West Coast. One asked who I was sleeping with to get on the Opry so fast. It hurt so much I cried day and night. The girls called a party and invited Patsy [Cline]. They didn't know me and Patsy was friends. . . . Patsy called and told me to get my hair done. She bought me a new outfit and made me go. We went in there, and they didn't say a word. That ended their plan. Patsy put the stamp of approval on me, and I never had any problems again.

—LORETTA LYNN, 1993

[The other performers] were very friendly to me, very supportive, and accepted me into the "family" immediately. I might add that I represented no threat to any of them. I didn't sing and I was a woman. Men, at that time, *never* figured a woman to be a threat.

—MINNIE PEARL (1912–1996), on playing the Grand Ole Opry, 1993

I was 12. . . . I sang "Lovesick Blues" with [Ernest Tubb's] Texas Troubadours backin' me. I was underage—you had to be 16 to play the Opry. But Daddy lied about my age, and Mama put these little inserts into my trainin' bra to make me look older.

—AUDREY WIGGINS, 1994

I feel this is a family here, so kinda regardless of whatever happens in your life, you always can come home to the Grand Ole Opry, thank God.   —RONNIE MILSAP, 1996

I imagine that some of the best music that has taken place has been backstage at the Ryman.

—JOHN BERRY, 1996

It's like a dream, that someday I'd get a chance to be part of country music and walk out on the [Ryman] stage and sing a song or two. And there's no greater feeling than performing on that stage. It's where country music, as we know it today, was born and nurtured and it's still alive within these walls.   —MARK COLLIE, 1996

There's an interesting phenomenon that happens with an old theater. I've heard people talk about it like fine wine. [Theaters get] warmer, they absorb all the vibrations, all the music that has been performed here. . . . It's still here. It's a real treat for a singer to work in a nice theater, because it enhances what you're tryin' to do, and it just makes it that much better for the audience.

—PAM TILLIS, on the Ryman Auditorium, 1996

We hear strange noises every night around 10:30 to 1:00, and people says there's ghosts in the auditorium.

—Ryman Auditorium security guard, 1996

LIFE ON THE ROAD

BACK IN THE SADDLE AGAIN

Back when we played the clubs and the bars, it could be said that you needed [a handgun], just to make sure you got paid your money at the end of the night.

—ALAN JACKSON, 1995

I don't like music in huge concert halls. To me that's just not the way to listen to music. . . . Little tight groups. Little sweaty places where you get packed in and you're truly a part of everything that's going on. That's the way to listen to music, I think.

—DELBERT McCLINTON, 1996

"Silent Night" proved to be my all-time lifesaver. Just when [bar fights] started getting out of hand, when bikers were reaching for their pool cues and rednecks were heading for the gun rack, I'd start playing "Silent Night." It could be the middle of July—I didn't care. Sometimes, I swear, they'd even start crying, standing there watching me sweat and play Christmas carols.

—TRAVIS TRITT, 1994

You're standin' up there playin', and somebody hits you in the back of the head with a beer bottle. Maybe not intendin' to . . . maybe he's throwin' it at his wife, or somethin'. Throws your timin' off.

—WILLIE NELSON, 1988

Gilley's was the all-time worst. I hate that fucking place. . . . The stage is only a few feet off the floor. We've played plenty of tough fucking beer joints, but we'd do a gig at Gilley's and come out with bruises and cuts and our shirts torn. People would be fistfighting in the crowd. Gilley's is a fucking skull orchard. You look out there at the crowd in that dim light and it's like a melon patch. People throwing shit. They could shoot each other without us even knowing it.

—RANDY LOCKE, Willie Nelson's stage manager, on Mickey Gilley's joint in Pasadena, Texas, made famous by the film *Urban Cowboy,* 1988

I was always scared in honky-tonks and dives and chicken-wire places when I played them. One time, one girl in a honky-tonk got real mad that her drunk husband was gettin' carried away. I guess she had some to drink, too. She yelled out, "Let me at that bitch! I'll get that wig offa her!" The band was gathering around to protect me. But bein' a country girl, I'd have taken her on if she'd got to me.   —DOLLY PARTON, 1993

I wanted them to notice me, so I got a 50-foot cord between the Strat [Stratocaster guitar] and the amp, and by the third or fourth set I was doing "Johnny B. Goode" from the top of one of the tables. I got fired from a lot of gigs.

—TRAVIS TRITT, on his early performances, 1994

[Bob Wills] would hit the bandstand at eight P.M. and stay for four hours without a break. One song would end, he'd count four and hit another one. . . . I learned from him to keep the people moving and dancing. That way, you don't lose their attention, plus your amplifiers drown out whatever the drunks might yell.

—WILLIE NELSON, 1988

Those people out there, when you [put on] a concert, they don't care if you've had a bad day. They don't care about your problems. In their eyes you are the luckiest, happiest, most successful person in the world, because this is what you do for a living. And that's the way it's supposed to be. . . . You've gotta get out there and take care of the crowd like it's the last time you're ever gonna get on that stage.   —TRACY LAWRENCE, 1995

That's one thing I learned from Buddy [Holly]. If you leave [the stage] when you're ahead, [the fans] exaggerate how good it was. But if you wait till it's all over, when you're starting to lose it, they'll exaggerate how bad it was. —WAYLON JENNINGS, 1982

It's like Roger Miller said, "You dazzle them and run."
—MARTY STUART, 1994

[It's] like great sex, where you get wild and frenzied, then turn that around real quick to something gentle, tender, and slow, and then get wild and crazy again and just keep doing that over and over until one of you drops dead.

—GARTH BROOKS, describing the exchange
between the audience and the performer, 1994

A long time ago when I walked onto a stage to do a show, I would search the room with my eyes. I was looking for somebody who was looking at me, who appeared interested in learning what I was doing in front of the microphone with a guitar in my hands. Once I found that friendly face, I would sing to that person all night long.

—WILLIE NELSON, 1988

You know, I don't even like to be up on a stage, really. I like to be where I can look at ya. I don't want to sing down to you. I want you to sing with me. —LORETTA LYNN

Every night when I hit that stage, I make sure I come out squawlin' tires! —AARON TIPPIN, 1995

~49

Every show is like Game Time! I have a saying, "All right, guys, it's time to hit the beach!" Kind of like the Normandy Invasion. It's fun to still be that excited about what you're doing.

—RANDY OWEN, of Alabama, 1994

On stage, you're just *pumped,* man. You can feel no pain. You could sprain an ankle out there and not even feel it. A lot of nights I come off the stage with my hands all cut up, or I've knocked a hole in my head against my guitar—or against somebody! It's a wild adrenaline rush.

—KIX BROOKS, of Brooks & Dunn, 1993

I have so much fun onstage that I should pay to get in.

—MARTY ROBBINS (1925–1982)

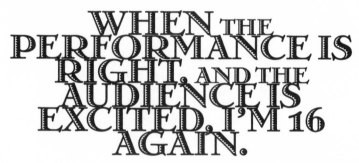

WHEN THE PERFORMANCE IS RIGHT, AND THE AUDIENCE IS EXCITED, I'M 16 AGAIN.

—CARL PERKINS

It's the scene in *Risky Business,* where Tom Cruise dances in his underwear. I just happen to have clothes on and do it in front of an audience.

—MARK MILLER, of Sawyer Brown, 1996

This whole concert bit is sort of weird to me. . . . They're doing rock concerts these days in [the country music] business. That's kinda hard for me to keep up with. I've got the stage, and all the computerized moving lights and this crap. . . . I mean, the whole deal is, you got two choices: you can either be Kiss, or you can be Mark Chesnutt.

—MARK CHESNUTT, 1995

When you're 14 or 15 years old and you think about being a rock star or a country singer, the thing you think about is being out onstage in front of screaming fans, beautiful women and throwing your sweat around. That's what I always thought about and that's the impetus that drives my career. —TIM McGRAW, 1996

I was going for the peak of the show, and everything dropped into slow motion. . . . I noticed the guy down front in the white shirt with maroon lettering and the maroon baseball cap, who was just going nuts. I noticed the little kid over there with his mom holding him up. I noticed the older lady who had been sitting down the whole show but was now standing up. I could see each individual. Everything was right in the sweet spot of the bat. I could feel it in my shoulders and in the joints of my elbows. And all of a sudden it felt like somebody had ahold of me, like a perfectly tailored suit. If I raised this arm, that side of the coliseum would rise with it—the seats, concrete, everything, would rise. . . . I know you're probably thinking, This fucker's nuts. But I shit you not; I felt it. And those seconds are why I go in the business.

—GARTH BROOKS, 1994

You go out and perform in front of live people, lookin' out at the faces, and it's real easy to come on and turn on. But in the studio it's just a bunch of old, ugly men. —NEAL McCOY, 1996

A song lasts for so long, that's a slow gratitude that you sip on. The live show is a shot of tequila! You get your bang for your buck.

—KIX BROOKS, of Brooks & Dunn, 1996

[After a show] my mind is running through a million things. And it's quiet. You *want* to hear that loud noise. You want to hear that crowd again. . . . It's like going cold turkey off a drug. It's cut off . . . just like that.

—TRAVIS TRITT, 1996

I've seen so many country acts . . . that will sing themselves right on top and then talk theirselves right into a hole and just bury it. . . . If you ain't got something that's funny, informative, or important, then shut up. —WAYLON JENNINGS, 1974

I can remember people like Roy Head and George Thorogood coming through the bars in Louisiana where I grew up and went to school. They were the kind of singers I really dug: the ones that'd jump on your table, kick your beer all over you, and keep boogyin'.

—KIX BROOKS, of Brooks & Dunn, 1993

I've always been personally drawn to artists who could just stand there and nail you to the wall with a great tune. Like Emmylou Harris used to. That's my deal. I'm still a little tentative as a performer.

—RONNIE DUNN, of Brooks & Dunn, 1993

You get up there in the spotlight and you can't really see the crowd, and I can hide under my hat.

—TIM McGRAW, on how he overcomes his shyness, 1995

I remember feeling this slow panic building inside me that the words weren't coming. I was just on automatic pilot, playing the chords, but no words. What I ended up doing was just repeating the first verse. . . . I remember I stood there for what seemed like a year. . . . It was terrible, as if I'd woke up one day and something I'd known how to do my whole life I didn't know how to do anymore. And once it's happened to you, you're always afraid it's gonna happen again.

—MARY CHAPIN CARPENTER, on stage fright, 1995

It still feels like I'm really out of character when I'm [onstage], because I'm constantly just freaked out. People tell me, "Well, you look so calm and confident out there." Well, it's an absolute facade.

—RONNIE DUNN, of Brooks & Dunn, 1994

It's funny how a chubby kid can just be having fun, and people call it entertainment.

—GARTH BROOKS

The worst thing that ever happened to [the band] was when we opened for Willie [Nelson] and only got to play 45 minutes. He got to play three hours and we only got to get drunk and watch.

—JERRY JEFF WALKER, 1994

If you really want to try something unusual, try passin' out in front of five thousand people. —LORETTA LYNN, 1993

The only [country stars] I ever saw that really needed a rest from *exhaustion* were Loretta Lynn and Tammy Wynette, bless their hearts. They had a reason to be tired. Other than that, I ain't felt sorry for a one of 'em. —JOHN ANDERSON, 1993

I am killin' myself [performing on the road]. But I'm havin' a good time doin' it. —BILLY RAY CYRUS, 1993

I used to do anything I wanted at the drop of a hat. I stayed up while others drank coffee to stay awake with me. I had an unlimited amount of energy all my life. . . . I can't do what I used to do. I'm using all I've got to get it done. I've learned if you pace yourself, you can still deliver come stage time.

—MERLE HAGGARD, 1996

The old saying "The show must go on" does not apply to me anymore. I've tried that. The show must go on as long as I'm able.

—TAMMY WYNETTE, on performing while sick, 1988

Your sanity is so much more important than just trying to turn a buck. —MARY CHAPIN CARPENTER, on taking time off, 1995

Living that kind of existence can be rough on a person. . . . [The road] liked to ruin my mind. —WAYLON JENNINGS, 1969

Ever see *The Man with Two Brains*? Steve Martin is looking at his dead wife's picture, and he says, "If there's some sign for me not to marry this girl, let me know." And the picture starts spinning and the wall cracks, shit's flying all over. Then it calms down and he says, "*Any* sign. I'll be looking for a sign." So yeah, I'll be looking for subtle hints.

—GARTH BROOKS, on knowing when it's time to stop performing, 1994

After about three months [on the road], we stopped asking where we were. There was the road, the road, and the road, a single endless ribbon that defined our days and nights.

—TRAVIS TRITT, 1994

What I dislike most is the traveling. The main trouble and danger, maybe, with tours, is getting there and back.

—JIM REEVES (1924–1964), one year before dying in an airplane crash

The road has taken a lot of people that I love . . . casualties. . . . I think about people like Roger Miller, Merle Watson, Clarence White, Keith Whitley, Hank Sr., all those kind of guys. Patsy Cline, Reba McEntire's band; the road claimed them. And so it's not just play time out here. It's serious business.

—MARTY STUART, 1996

I can't sleep in a bed that's not moving.   —TRACY LAWRENCE, 1994

I can't sleep anywhere but on the [tour] bus. They park it by my house and let me sleep in it all the time so I can get a good night's rest.   —TIM MCGRAW, 1996

The bus is probably the most important instrument in country music.   —BARBARA MANDRELL

IT'S MY NATURAL HABITAT.

—LEE ROY PARNELL, on the road, 1994

The two hours you're on the stage is what you live for when you're on the road, but the other 22 are boring.

—JOHNNY CASH, 1989

It's a shame that it takes so long on the road to have those few incredible minutes with the audience.   —DON WILLIAMS, 1994

It's hard to keep your head up all the time when you're traveling and all you see is the roof of some motel room and an audience full of strange faces. I guess the impersonal part gets to me.

—WAYLON JENNINGS, 1972

I was 12 years old when I went on the road the first time. What I learned about the road and what I love about it is the same thing now as then: it's free.   —MARTY STUART, 1996

Playing the road is just like robbing Wells Fargo. You ride in, take the money, and ride out.   —MARTY ROBBINS (1925–1982)

The Road [was] *the* legendary, let-it-all-hang-out location for every dedicated, wild-ass, manic-depressive, amphetamine-crazed hill-billy singer: a no man's land, where one was free from petty moral restraints and nagging wives and girlfriends; a pleasure-seeker's par-adise where one could, if one chose, subsist for weeks on whiskey, beer, Benzedrine, coffee, cigarettes, stale bacon, lettuce, and tomato sandwiches and lots of *eezy luuuuuvin'*.

—BOB ALLEN, journalist, 1994

I like the camaraderie of a band, the brotherhood of being on the road. Being in a band is sort of like high school with money. We're out there to have a ball.   —LEE ROY PARNELL, 1994

[Waylon Jennings, Willie Nelson, Kris Kristofferson and I] have 120 years of friendship and 137 years of road work [combined], and let me tell you that the friendship is the best. Sometimes it can be sheer hell out there on the road.

—JOHNNY CASH, 1996

We may play a two-and-a-half-hour show in a club, and once we've got on dry clothes and gotten on the bus and are rolling down the highway, we might play for another two hours for ourselves. That's not unusual for us. —LEE ROY PARNELL, 1994

Pushing yourself to go on the road, that gets in the way of thinking. . . . I'm prone to want to be in a very consistent environment. I like continuity. And touring 33 out of 48 months is very debilitating to me personally, because I can't write in that environment of motion. —DWIGHT YOAKAM, 1993

I went [on the road] with Waylon [Jennings] and a few buddies like Buck Owens, so I knew how the road was, and I never really liked it. I hate driving. Those 500-mile jumps every day could get real old real fast to me. So I just said I'll write songs and let them sing 'em. —HARLAN HOWARD, 1994

One day you get up at four-thirty and the next day you get up at noon. The next day you have to leave right after the show at 11 o'clock and catch a plane, so that at four in the morning you're sitting in Chicago for two hours to save money on plane flights. You fly out again at six A.M. and you arrive at eight A.M. and you spend half an hour waiting for your rent-a-cars with your eyes bleeding all over the airport floor.

—LACY J. DALTON

You must tour The Road! And the road means you must talk to at least X number of people a day. Meet and greet and [they say], "Hi! We don't like you, but our dry-cleaner does, and we're here to look you in the face and tell him later what you look like."

—K. T. OSLIN, 1993

I'll tell you what I like about being on the road. I don't know if I'm just superstitious about this, but I tend to think that if I get to a town and take a walk, meet some people, talk to somebody . . . the shows seem to be better.

—RODNEY CROWELL, 1996

[Touring is] not really that much work to me. I enjoy doin' it. If I didn't play music, if I wasn't allowed to play music, I'd probably get physically sick. It's just something I have to do.

—WILLIE NELSON, 1988

> # WHEN I COME HOME [FROM THE ROAD] I'M LOST AND CAN'T FIND MY UNDERCLOTHES.
> —LORETTA LYNN, 1978

I remember one day not long ago I came home from a long road trip, and my three-year-old son asked my wife, "Mommy, is he spending the night here tonight?"

—RONNIE DUNN, of Brooks & Dunn, 1993

Do you know where wives come from? Wives come from the fourth row [of the audience]. . . . After the show you have somebody invite her backstage. All the guys are enormously friendly to her, light her cigarettes, open the doors for her, say, "Yes ma'am. So you invite her on the bus and she thinks this is the most romantic thing in her whole life. This goes on for about three months—or until you marry her, whichever comes first. Suddenly nobody lights her cigarettes or opens her door or pays her the slightest damn bit of attention anymore. She starts thinking, God, I've got to get off the road, this is horrible, I want a house and a place to sit. . . . This lasts about three more months. Then it all turns to shit. [She's home thinking], "It would all be perfect if that sorry no-good son of a bitch out on the road was sitting here with me."

—WILLIE NELSON, 1988

In order to play [guitar] well, you've got to play a lot. In order to sing well, you have to sing a lot. . . . you need to be out there. Now I've moved into a period of my life that I understand the only way

I can continue to perform and maintain a level of excellence is by performing all the time and staying in real good shape.

—MERLE HAGGARD, 1996

Every night now I start getting a little antsy. I'm starting to remember the feel of the stage grating beneath my feet again. I'm remembering what the smell is like of getting into an empty hall for the sound check. I'm getting ready for it.

—GARTH BROOKS, on ending his musical leave of absence, 1996

[My old tour bus] was Ernest Tubb's bus. I loved that machine. It was the last of the great hillbilly buses. Ernest and his Texas Troubadours rode mile after mile on it—the old man basically ended his career on it. . . . We finally wore it out. So to show my love and respect for it, the last thing I did was to shoot two holes right through the back-room floor. It was a proper way to say good-bye. I put it out of its misery, like an old warhorse.

—MARTY STUART, 1996

When I was coming up [in country music], you weren't a bona fide country star until you had a [tour] bus with your name written in big letters on the side. My first bus in 1962 was a used, dented, and rusty contraption, with bare sheet-metal walls inside. My band, the Jones Boys, called it "the gas chamber." Diesel fumes seeped through the floor into the cabin and it had no air-conditioning. Have you ever traveled in solid steel across a steaming highway with a hot engine in the summertime?

—GEORGE JONES, 1996

HERE IN THE REAL WORLD ===

They gotta shop at Wal-Mart, just like the rest of us.

—CONFEDERATE RAILROAD, on the major requirement for being a band member, 1995

Patsy may have been a celebrity elsewhere, but at home they were used to her. She'd walk up and down the streets with her hair in rollers and no one paid any mind.

—HILDA HENSLEY, Patsy Cline's mother, 1993

When we come off the road, we've got all this energy *from* the road. We got careers, we've got people pulling at us, we've got this, like, constant demand to be performers. Yet, we realize that we're at home; we're not these performers. Trisha is just Trisha . . . *Patricia.* And I'm just Robert.

—ROBERT REYNOLDS, lead singer of the Mavericks and Trisha Yearwood's husband, 1996

When I go home I don't get up every day and wash my hair, and blow-dry it, and put on leather jeans and fringe jackets. I get up and throw on a ready pair of blue jeans and put on a baseball cap and get on my tractor and mow hay. —TRAVIS TRITT, 1994

Yesterday I worked in the yard at my farm up in the country. I hoed my tomatoes, my okry. I dug around my roses, set out some fig bushes, worked around my grape vines. I do that kind of stuff. That's my therapy. —JOHNNY CASH, 1996

I want to sit on my front porch and yell at the kids, "Hey! Get out of my yard!" —K. T. OSLIN, 1993

I just want to make some real good music, and make some real good money, and buy a farm with enough space around me so that I don't have to be starin' at the neighbors taking a bath. Or so I can sit naked on my front porch in a rocking chair. And praise the Lord and pass the jar. —LACY J. DALTON, 1988

When I'm home I'm thinking about being on the road. When I'm on the road for a month, it'll get a little hectic. I start getting home-sick and aggravated about things. I'll think about all the things I'll do when I get home. Basically, nothing. —MARK CHESNUTT, 1996

On the road everything is regimented—when I get up, when I do interviews, when I perform. At home, all that goes in the crapper. I don't pay attention to what time I get up. Sometimes my alarm clock goes off because it's still set from the last time I was home. I've been known to smash an alarm clock or two.

—TRAVIS TRITT, 1994

[Home is] up on a mountain. It's out in the middle of nowhere. You get here and it gives you what you need to get back out *there*.

—TRISHA YEARWOOD, 1996

God gave me this gift [of music], and if I want to take a stinkin' year and a half off, I can.

—WYNONNA JUDD, on taking a break from performing, 1996

It was a good break for my family and myself. And to give [fans] a break from us. Give them a breath.

—GARTH BROOKS, on taking time off, 1996

THIS MUSIC THING IS GETTING IN THE WAY OF MY GOLF GAME.

—VINCE GILL, 1993

I was a housewife and mother for 15 years before I was an entertainer. And it wasn't like being a housewife today. I mean, it was hand laundry and cookin' on an old coal stove. . . . When I slow down I'll do it again. —LORETTA LYNN, 1993

A lot of women will probably think I'm crazy, but I enjoy just cleaning up around the house and getting my hands into things. It's work for some, but I don't look at it as work. I look at it as something that's helping me to ease my mind. —PATTY LOVELESS, 1994

If I never have another hit record, if I bomb tomorrow, I'll sit at home, have a new truck, and fish, and I'll have everything I need to sustain me. —TRAVIS TRITT, 1994

My family, my collection of old trucks and [bull]dozers, that's all just something to keep my hands in the world of the same folks I go out and play for. —AARON TIPPIN, 1995

I've always enjoyed being alone. I've never had a problem with talking to myself, because some of my best conversations are between me and just my own self cruising down the highway.
—WILLIE NELSON, 1988

It's really as simple as visiting some other people in the town where you are, or settin' by a river and getting yourself slowed down enough to listen. —MARTY STUART, on taking time out to do some soul-searching, 1995

Volunteerism is something that goes back to helping a fellow when his barn burns down, or helping a fellow that falls out of the loft and breaks his leg to feed his cattle and take care of his children. It's basic; it's fundamental, and I think most people feel that way.
—MINNIE PEARL (1912–1996)

I lost a fortune on pigs. I had the fattest pigs in town, or in the country. I paid 25 cents a pound for 'em and fattened 'em up for six months. When I sold 'em, I got 17 cents a pound for 'em. Lost my ass and all its fixtures. —WILLIE NELSON, on his early-career hiatus, 1988

I haven't seen [Marty's] hog lately. I think it's up to 500 or 600 pounds, and I don't think it can make it over the hill anymore. But you know which one it is 'cause Marty painted his phone number on its side. When you see a hog with a phone number on it, it's an awesome sight.   —TOM T. HALL, on his neighbor Marty Stuart, 1993

I CAN STILL BUILD SOME OF THE PRETTIEST HOUSES YOU'LL EVER SEE.
—SAMMY KERSHAW, on his talents as a carpenter, 1993

She's the only constant female in my life.

—MERLE HAGGARD, praising his Chihuahua, Tuffy

I love fox hounds. I love to hear 'em run as they give their mouths, as they bark behind the fox. There's a lot of dogs that's got wonderful mouths. They got a high tenor voice or a deep sharp, or they'd bark like a turkey, or some had screamin' mouths. . . . Put 'em all together, it makes a wonderful sound.

—BILL MONROE (1911–1996), 1982

I've never been a fan of hunting. Probably never will be. We had a .22 rifle which we kept in the house, but that was all. It was never in my blood and I never want it to be. I'll go fishing, but most of the time I'll throw back what I catch or I'll eat it. I don't really believe in killing for the sake of it.   —ALAN JACKSON, 1995

THE FANS: ALL I EVER NEED IS YOU

I ask all the young ladies in the audience to give a holler, all by themselves. And then when they do, I tell them how much I appreciate it, even if I *did* have to ask for it.

—MERLE HAGGARD, 1995

If a man is sexy, that doesn't offend the men in the crowd. They know the women are just having fun. But if a gal is sexy and something of a come-on, the women in the audience take offense. They don't want their husbands or their boyfriends seeing that.

—REBA McENTIRE, 1993

It's kind of easy to not mess with [groupies]. Personally, I got that out of my system a long time ago. Back when we were playing in the clubs. I could stay in one town for five days straight. There were four single guys in the band then, so we'd milk the club dry after five days and we enjoyed every pleasant-looking young lady that there was to be looked at in the club . . . but that was the old days.

—DUANE PROPES, of Little Texas, 1995

Beautiful women I thought were unreal would walk up to me and say, "Sign this." Only there was nothing in their hands. So I just dove in and had a blast.

—GARTH BROOKS, 1993

[A fan] came up and showed me she had my name tattooed on her breast. I asked her husband what he thought of that, and the woman said, "Oh, it's all right. He's got 'Lorrie Morgan' tattooed on his butt."

—MARTY STUART, 1996

In Milwaukee, some gal walked up to the stage. . . . She took her blouse off and threw it up to Kix to sign. . . . We get the jumping up onstage and the moshing thing—driving back into the crowd. It's wild. —RONNIE DUNN, of Brooks & Dunn, 1996

I don't think my fan base looks at me as a heartthrob like some of these other guys. I've got a little bit of Gomer in me.
—VINCE GILL, 1994

You can't date fans, because fans look at you as larger than life. It's not a lot of fun to go out on a date with someone who's starin' at you like she's waiting for you to walk across the swimming pool.
—TRAVIS TRITT, 1994

Take a helicopter they can land any place that is the only way you can come and get me. You can see a big field the field is on 19 mile road. . . . Come at night so know will see me go with you I need about 4 or 5 men to carry out the 5 boxes and a hat box. If you do not want me give this litter to Johnny Cash.
—A fan letter to Bill Anderson, 1970

That's the first woman who could make me feel like crying out of one eye and winking out of the other. —A Patsy Cline fan, 1993

I have just as many men fans, because in my songs I say things that men want to say but most men have trouble saying . . . things that women like to hear. This way, all the men have to do is drop a quarter in the jukebox and play the song. It's letting Conway say it for you. —CONWAY TWITTY (1933–1993)

My shows are really geared to women fans . . . to the hard-working housewife who's afraid some girl down at the factory is going to steal her husband, or wishing she could bust out of her shell a little bit.
—LORETTA LYNN, 1993

I wish you could see the letters I get; they are so precious. I'm like the den mother of country music.
—TRISHA YEARWOOD, on her young, female fan base, 1993

Liking country is suddenly hip. The younger generation will be our audience for the next 10 years. They can relate to what I sing about. . . . It's something that happens to them everyday.

—REBA McENTIRE, 1993

I'M NOT QUITTING TILL THE FANS SAY I'M THROUGH.

—DOUG STONE, after quadruple-bypass heart surgery, 1993

We were always a little mystified why 40 million people would watch Louise, Irlene, and me cavorting around onstage.

—BARBARA MANDRELL

I've had big hits, mediocre hits, and now I've got no hits at all, but most of my fans are still with me.

—BILLY "CRASH" CRADDOCK, 1996

That's the beautiful thing about country music. Once somebody becomes a fan, they'll stay right with you until you're 70.

—CONWAY TWITTY (1933–1993)

There's a new rock group every five minutes, but with country music, you have one hit and those people love you forever.

—KENNY ROGERS, 1980

From watching Lester [Flatt], I learned that it's important to be loyal to the people who made you and bought your music. He called me up to the front of the [tour] bus on the very first trip I went on with him. Lester pointed out two elderly people who were walking towards the bus. He said, "Those two people have been coming to see me since the mid-40s. That's what a country fan is all about."

—MARTY STUART, 1994

~65

[The fans] might be walking a country mile to get to the show. . . . They save up their money, and they get there and . . . no George. It breaks my heart now that I realize this and think about it.

—GEORGE JONES, on failing to show for concerts, 1995

I never thought I was worth comin' to see—I was hostile to my audiences and had to drink to get myself on the stage to face them. I got into an "us against them" situation, which is ridiculous. I'm surprised I've got a fan left.　　　　—KRIS KRISTOFFERSON, 1977

I'M NOT A MAJOR TALENT. I'M A PRODUCT OF THE PEOPLE.
—GARTH BROOKS

We want to say to the people, "You've changed us, and I hope you see yourselves in us. Because you made us. . . ." The fans have validated me.　　　　—NAOMI JUDD, 1993

This may sound corny, but for me the bottom line is that handshake, that hug, that "My child goes to sleep to your music." One of the reasons I kept going [after Naomi retired] was the fans.

—WYNONNA JUDD, 1994

I love singing and I love my fans. Their applause is a narcotic. . . . It's the best drug in the world. And right now it's legal.

—TRACY BYRD, 1996

The fans are wonderful, they're sweet, they're kind. There's nothing easier than being around fans.　　　　—SHANIA TWAIN, 1995

[The fans] bring us baked goods to the show—candies, cookies, cakes, chocolate. Want to see how big my butt has gotten?

—LORIANNE CROOK, of Nashville's talk-music show *Crook and Chase*, 1996

God love 'em. They'll do anything for you but leave you alone.

—MARTY ROBBINS (1925–1982)

Me, my friend Evelyn, and our husbands went to see Marty Robbins and Faron Young perform in Ashville. Marty's "White Sport Coat and a Pink Carnation" had just come out. I remember him wearing that same outfit onstage. When Evelyn and I went to the rest room, there was Marty Robbins and Faron Young walkin' down the hallway. Faron wasn't so flirty, but Marty had a fit over Evelyn. Said he had never seen anything like her in all his life. . . . He was so in love, I had a time getting her away from him. And he was about six inches shorter than she was.   —LOUISE STOCKTON, a fan

I love country music fans. They're truly the most loyal fans that any form of music could ever hope to have. About all it takes is to hang out with 'em, hug their neck, sign their pictures. Which works both ways, 'cause sometimes you step off the bus, you feel like you can't go another day—and they send back that love and that energy. When somebody walks up and says, "I love you." That's the ultimate, and better than anything else they could give you. I don't think it costs anything to treat people good.   —MARTY STUART, 1996

Up until the last show [Ernest Tubb] ever did, when he was so sick he couldn't breathe sometimes, when he got done with that show, he would go to the edge of the stage, set down in a chair, take pictures, whatever [the fans] wanted. And he would not leave until everyone got an autograph.   —JUSTIN TUBB, Ernest Tubb's son, 1996

I think taking the time to meet the fans is the most important thing in anybody's career. They're the ones who make it happen. If they quit supporting you, then you don't have a lot left.

—CLINTON GREGORY, country fiddle player

[The fans would] come to the bus after the show, and they'd ask to talk to me. They felt I had the answer to their problems because my life was just like theirs. . . . I ain't Dear Abby. I had a few problems maybe *they* could have solved for me.   —LORETTA LYNN, 1993

I was in Nordstrom's once, trying a dress on. I'm in my underwear, and this lady slips this piece of paper under the door. "Can you sign this?"　—MARY CHAPIN CARPENTER, 1995

LONG BEFORE I WAS A STAR, I WAS A FAN.

—BILL ANDERSON

When I work my booth at Fan Fair and I see all of the people in line wanting my autograph, I then look around the room and see all the stars that I want to meet. If I wasn't doing what I was doing, I'd be in line at the other booths.　—LINDA DAVIS, 1996

We're backing off a lot from the kind of stuff like signing autographs for 15 hours at Fan Fair. Because I've hit 40, and I'm getting too old for that. I don't want to put my fans through that, either, because they're loyal and they'll sit there for 15 hours.

—REBA McENTIRE, 1996

[Autographs are] actually a courtesy thing on the part of the artists, if you want to know the way I feel about it. . . . A lot of people say you owe it to them, but somebody once said, and it's true, that all you owe the people is a good performance, 'cause that's what they paid to hear. You don't owe them your soul.　—WAYLON JENNINGS, 1985

I never did cater to the autograph set. They make up about four percent of all the people who come to the show. And they're the people who want more than their ticket gives 'em. And if you gave it to them, they'd want somethin' else.　—MERLE HAGGARD

Never think of yourself as any bigger than the man who's buying the ticket to see you.　—TENNESSEE ERNIE FORD (1919–1991)

People don't come to the shows to see you be you. They come to see you be *them,* and what they want to be.　—DOLLY PARTON, 1993

"Garth" just lies there in powder form till the music comes up, and the people come up. —GARTH BROOKS, 1995

The only thing that makes a hit is whether or not it clicks with the audience. And you never know that till you get done.

—TRAVIS TRITT, 1994

Never forget that the American audience is essentially moral and sentimental. —EDDY ARNOLD

People for various reasons . . . will get tired of you. If you're not out there selling something that people feel they have to have almost as a necessity, they'll walk off on you in a second.

—RONNIE DUNN, of Brooks & Dunn, 1994

I don't make my music for Travis Tritt or anybody else. I make my music for myself and my fans. From what I've seen on the road, there's an awful lot of "Achy Breaky Heart" fans out there. The people of the world have made their decision, and that's all that matters to me.

—BILLY RAY CYRUS, responding to Travis Tritt's comment that Cyrus is turning country music into an "ass-wigglin'" contest, 1993

Sorry if I stammered when I met you, but I'm just like other girls, just a little older.

—A note from Dolly Parton to Billy Ray Cyrus, 1993

People use your music as the backdrop for everyday life. They live to your music, they work to it, they fall in love to it. But it's more than just attaching to the music. They attach to the person.

—WYNONNA JUDD, 1994

Fans bring experiences from their own lives that allow them to draw something extraordinary and personal from a song.

—KENNY BEARD, songwriter, 1996

I have a whole audience that really doesn't know my music. They know me as a celebrity, so to speak, a tabloid queen.

—TANYA TUCKER

These people know you through your music, and if they think you're thinking about going fishing or playing football while you're singing a great love song . . . it's like a woman layin' there eatin' an apple if you're makin' love to her. It's going to take something out of it. —CONWAY TWITTY (1933–1993)

Music is a way of communicating with the audience. If you can't sign an autograph or shake a hand, or even just sit down in conversation and hear a story, at least maybe you can share a part of yourself through songs. —PATTY LOVELESS, 1996

When you open your heart to an audience, you share your deepest feelings with them. They want to find love in your heart. They don't want to see that it's nothing but a bank vault. —WILLIE NELSON, 1988

I think I learned what [fans] want, what really makes them happy. Which is real simple, and not something that demographic statistics or anything else can figure out. They just want people who sing to them genuinely. If you can do that, I think they're gonna give you all the love you need to keep you going. —SUZY BOGGUSS, 1993

> # WHEN I QUIT MAKIN' RECORDS, MY [CONCERT] ATTENDANCE WENT UP.
> —MERLE HAGGARD, 1995

I'm the Susan Lucci of country music, but that's okay, 'cause people like me. And the applause . . . the applause from the crowd when I walk onstage and that standing ovation that I get, night after night; those are my awards. —CONWAY TWITTY (1933–1993)

Like everyone says, it's great to be nominated [for awards]. . . . But while some people might not want to admit it, I will! I want to win! —KIX BROOKS, of Brooks & Dunn, 1996

THE BIZ

3

SILVER THREADS AND GOLDEN NEEDLES

I've never been at the top. There's always somebody out there that's better, faster, wittier, and does something that sells more tickets or albums or is more popular. I've always been a bridesmaid.
                                                    —REBA McENTIRE, 1993

I'm not trying to be number one. I'm not trying to be the greatest. Once you're there, then what?
                                                    —WAYLON JENNINGS, 1983

As a teenager I dreamed about being in coliseums trying to catch the winning touchdown. When it came to music, I never saw the crowds of people. I just wanted to get my music out there. . . . I wanted to be an artist the American people could relate to. I wanted to be America's guy.
                                                    —GARTH BROOKS, 1994

People see someone famous and shy and they assume she's snooty. But the truth is I was dying inside to be loved and wanted.
                                                    —WYNONNA JUDD, 1996

I went to a McDonald's to eat and I was mobbed. That was the day my career went from teeter to totter.
                                                    —BILLY RAY CYRUS, 1993

I can't go home and turn off the fact that I'm a recognizable figure. I'm Travis Tritt, Country Singer. I have signed autographs at the grocery store in the middle of the night. It goes with the territory.
                                                    —TRAVIS TRITT, 1994

I can't bitch or complain. It's been a good run for me.
                                                    —GARTH BROOKS, 1996

Normally, I don't like songs about being in the music business. . . . People don't want to hear you sing about feeling sorry for yourself when you're riding around in a bus that costs more than their house. . . . To them, what we do for a living—though hard as it is— is very glamorous. It's very glamorous to me. I enjoy my job.

—STEVE EARLE, 1996

Personally, I don't understand how single individuals who are extremely popular deal with all of this [attention].

—DUANE PROPES, of Little Texas, 1995

Popularity . . . it's a great problem to have. But anybody who's never been through this can never understand the workload that comes with it. Out [on the road], it never ends. And when we finally do get back home to Nashville for a day or two, there's a hundred phone messages waiting. The last time I was home, my wife told me, "When you're gone, the phone never rings. But as soon as you get here, it never stops!"

—MARTY ROE, of Diamond Rio, 1993

[Our children] would much rather have us at home, but all they have, and things like their college educations, rely on us going out on the road and selling albums.

—RONNIE DUNN, of Brooks & Dunn, 1996

The kids are the ones who make the sacrifices. They pay the price for our stardom.   —KIX BROOKS, of Brooks & Dunn, 1996

I don't like being recognized. When I'm in a grocery store or at the post office or something, it makes me feel like I've got something on the back of my dress. It's not a pleasant feeling.

—ROSANNE CASH, 1993

Lately, I've started to have to pay the consequences of [fame]. I've had people starting . . . to show up on my doorstep . . . and it really scares me. That's a by-product of all this I could never have imagined.   —MARY CHAPIN CARPENTER, 1993

I know it's a part of fame. People who don't know me want to hurt me.

—LORRIE MORGAN, 1995

FAME IS AN OCCUPATIONAL HAZARD.

—ROSANNE CASH

Sometimes it's all overwhelming, but it's nothin' I'd give back.

—FAITH HILL, 1995

It's been great to be Merle Haggard. I'd have to be totally crazy not to be appreciative and in awe of my own life. I'm afraid to breathe; I'm afraid somethin's gonna happen.

—MERLE HAGGARD, 1995

One of the things about the business I've always found weird, extremely weird, is going onstage and being in front of seven, eight, nine, ten thousand people one minute, and five minutes later, literally, you're in a hotel room, alone, with nothing but silence all around you.

—TRAVIS TRITT, 1994

I keep thinking somebody's going to realize who I am, come up behind and tap me on the shoulder and say, "You gotta leave." I do know enough to know [fame] is going to go away one day.

—JEFF FOXWORTHY, comic, 1996

You know that old sayin' "You can never go back"? That's hogwash. I don't think there's a door behind me that's closed, and if [fame] dried up tomorrow, I could . . . still run a tractor, a crawler, a dump truck, and I could still fly an airplane. And I could still write a song. You can go back—you've just gotta want to.

—AARON TIPPIN, 1996

If Barbara Walters was interviewing *me*, I'd figure her career was as dead as mine.

—TOM T. HALL, 1993

When Glen Campbell [called me] "the feller with the little glasses and the big boots," then I knew I was in trouble.

—LOUIS MARSHALL "GRANDPA" JONES,
on his 1978 induction into the Hall of Fame, 1995

I hate the star part of the business. I like the singing and writing and all that goes with it. But I wish when I get off the [tour] bus I could be more normal and go down to Kmart and buy me a fishing lure. —ALAN JACKSON, 1996

We're shrinking down to Andy Warhol's 15 minutes of fame. "Stars" come and go quickly. —TRAVIS TRITT, 1994

I don't know that I've ever thought of myself as being famous. Words like "star" and "superstar" and all that, I think they're just words. —BRENDA LEE, 1993

I ain't no star. A star is something up in the night sky. People say to me, "You're a legend." I'm not a legend. I'm just a woman.

—LORETTA LYNN

A child asked one time for my autograph, and I said, "Why do you want it?" And she said, "'Cause you're a celebrity." And I told her, "The neighbor you have next door to you that's kind and good to his family, makes an honest living, brings it all home, and takes care of his family . . . he's a celebrity." —MINNIE PEARL (1912–1996)

We're actually pretty normal people, and we're actually better at being normal people then perhaps being celebrities.

—ROBERT REYNOLDS, of the Mavericks, on himself and his wife, Trisha Yearwood, 1996

We probably work as hard at being normal as we do anything else. I think that's when we feel real honest about doing the kind of music we do and singing about the things we sing about.

—MARK MILLER, of Sawyer Brown, 1996

I think people realize that I'm just a bum who got lucky. I believe that the one gift I have been granted is that I am the common dude.

I truly think that what I believe in, the majority of the people believe in as well.   —GARTH BROOKS, 1996

The first time I got asked to do *Lifestyles of the Rich and Famous,* I cracked up laughing and refused to do it. Check my refrigerator for Brie, and see if you can get those Playmates out of the pool!
     —TRAVIS TRITT, 1994

I still like to pee off the porch now and then. There's nothing like peeing on those snobs in Beverly Hills.   —DOLLY PARTON, 1984

> # I'VE GOT A NEW FORD TRACTOR AND A HOUSE THAT'S PAID FOR. WHAT ELSE DO YOU NEED?
> —TOM T. HALL, 1995

I've got a custom-built Stutz, a Rolls, a Mercedes, a Ferrari, a Corvette, and a station wagon, but I've only got a three-car garage.
     —KENNY ROGERS, 1988

You don't need five Cadillacs! It amazes me how people can do that and still call themselves country music singers. I mean, here's some guy says he's milked 15 cows since sunup, and he's got a 15-carat diamond ring on his hand!   —MARTY BROWN, 1993

I don't want to get rich, I just want to live good.
     —PATSY CLINE (1932–1963)

If [Patsy Cline] wanted money, it was for some kid down the street who needed clothing for school, or a neighbor who couldn't pay a doctor bill. I honestly believe that if Patsy had all the money in the world, she'd have divided it equally among all its people, and left herself with only enough for bus fare.
     —DONN HECHT, songwriter, 1993

There would be hobos come in the back door [of the places he played], and [Jimmie Rodgers] would say, "Let 'em come on in. Let 'em eat somethin'. I'm gonna give 'em ten dollars to go get somethin' to wear and a suitcase." He had the biggest heart I know of.

—JIMMIE DALE COURT, Jimmie Rodgers's grandson, 1996

I don't know what humanitarian really means. I guess it means that somewhere along the line you tried and maybe [in] a few places succeeded . . . I hope. [Humanitarian] sounds awful ambitious . . . awful grand, too much so.

—MINNIE PEARL (1912–1996), who has herself been called a humanitarian countless times

You can't take a poor fellow, take him out of a pair of overalls and dress him in a three-piece sharkskin suit, set him in a Fleetwood Cadillac with a gold record fixin' to come and a royalty check that's bigger than what the bank has in that little town he was raised in, and expect that dude to stay like he was. —CARL PERKINS

My friends, the people close to me, keep me grounded, so I don't get caught up in the star trip, the vainness of it all. . . . When you're very famous, when people you don't know are crazy about you and your music, it's a satisfying feeling, but it's also . . . well, I've seen it affect some people I've known. I've seen it turn a really nice, well-meaning kind of individual into a monster. —MARK COLLIE, 1996

This ain't a proper job. It's strange. It doesn't feel like work. I've become kinda spoiled. Sometimes all I have to do is turn up; everything else has been done. —ALAN JACKSON, 1995

I wanted fame more than money, because fame meant recognition for what you did. There was a place inside me that always wondered, you know, will I never make my mark on this world, what am I here for? —BOBBIE CRYNER, 1996

Money doesn't buy happiness, but it's nice to know I don't have to borrow money from my MasterCard to pay my Visa.

—TRAVIS TRITT, 1995

Two real luxuries in life are [flying] first class and having fresh-cut flowers. —MAC DAVIS, 1980

I finally got this thing figured out: the more records you sell, the more guitars you can buy. —MARTY STUART, 1994

I HAVE ALL THE MATERIAL THINGS I NEED AND A COUPLE I DON'T.

—WILLIE NELSON, 1980

I knew I'd made it when I had a stranger training my dog for eight months. —KRIS KRISTOFFERSON, 1977

Sometimes I think, "Boy, it's got to be a sin to do something that you love so much, and to get paid this kind of money for it." You know, when another guy's out there on an assembly line, working at something he doesn't like. He ought to be paid way more than me, because he suffers. I feel funny about that sometimes.

—CONWAY TWITTY (1933–1993)

I just realized that y'all are gonna pay me more money for strummin' one chord then I use to make in two weeks pitchin' pineapples.

—JOHN GERRARD, songwriter for Crook and Chase, of *Music City Tonight*, 1995

I remember thinking a few years ago that if someone would give me $5,000 I could own the world. —JOE DIFFIE, 1995

Twenty five years ago I even doubted whether I'd still be around, let alone thought about what I'd be doing. I can jump in a car, tune in [to the radio], and I'll be there. I never had anything like that before. It's great that I got to wait around long enough [for that to happen]. —JOHN PRINE, 1995

~79

When you hear [your own songs] in your truck or your car, it sounds 15 times better than when you hear it on a CD, because when it's on the radio it's somebody else choosing to play it.

—GARTH BROOKS, 1996

I made a decision early that I would either be a beach bum with the freedom of roaming around without money in my pocket, being a writer or whatever, or I was going to do it with money in the bank and do it first class.

—BILLY DEAN, 1993

I'm at a point where I've had such success in the music business that I really want to savor it. I've spent a lot of time manifesting and pushing and creating and visualizing this gig. And now I've got this gig; I get to be Hal Ketchum. It's a wonderful place to be.

—HAL KETCHUM, 1996

Three years ago would you have thought that the largest-selling artist in the '90s would be going bald and have an eating problem and be doing fiddle and steel-guitar music?

—GARTH BROOKS, on his unusual success, 1994

We are digging our toe in the dirt about [our success]. We don't know what we did, so we don't know what to do next. That thing is an equal part of "aw, shucks" and hard work. We did it for 20 years without making any dough at all. And if the dough stopped, we would just keep doing it. We already know how to do it broke-wise!

—STEVE RIPLEY, of the Tractors, 1995

WHAT KEEPS ME GOING? THE FEAR OF STARVING.
—LEE ROY PARNELL

I started out even. It took me 30 years to get five million in debt.

—MERLE HAGGARD, 1994

Bob [Wills] finally died broke. I don't think it really bothered him to go out like that. He saw plenty of money in his life, but he didn't try to take it with him. Probably he intends to come back and get it.

—WILLIE NELSON, 1988

I've always been real conservative when it comes to spending money. You get a big check today doesn't mean you get a big check tomorrow.

—TRAVIS TRITT, 1994

If I was in this business to make a dollar, I'd 'a quit a long time ago.

—LEE ROY PARNELL, 1996

Success, to me, is doing something you love to do and being able to make a living at it. It's not measured in how much money you make. It's measured in mental freedom and happiness, being happy with your life, no matter what it is.

—CONWAY TWITTY (1933–1993)

I'm not sure [stars are] suppose to be too happy. It's never been that way for me. I've had things that people would surely gauge as being great that didn't excite me at all. And things that were the most important to me were the ones that people never could understand.

—MERLE HAGGARD, 1988

My life right now is where I've always wished it would be. The heavenly bodies have aligned. . . . This is just another piece of pie I don't deserve—but I'll eat it anyway.

—GARTH BROOKS, 1996

By luck and perseverance, I've come to a pretty good place, and get to do what I like for a living. Life keeps getting better, and [me and my band] can't believe we keep getting away with it.

—KRIS KRISTOFFERSON, 1977

You spend your life workin' for [success], and I know there's folks who'd trade with me any day, but there are still things I miss.

—ALAN JACKSON, 1995

TO ME, SUCCESS IS NOT REALLY DOLLARS. IT'S OPTIONS.

—KENNY ROGERS, 1981

[Success is] anyone who gets to play music and eat.

—WILLIE NELSON, 1980

Success is not getting what you want, it's enjoying what you have.

—GLEN CAMPBELL, 1980

Success is having to worry about every damned thing in the world except money.   —JOHNNY CASH, 1993

This ain't about being a hard worker. This is about being great. A great songwriter or a great singer or a great musician. It's not about how hard you try. I want to hear the old boys like George Jones who don't have to *try.* The people that have to try need jobs in the Holiday Inn lounges.   —JOHN ANDERSON, 1993

People do treat you different when you're successful. As we get older, regardless of whatever kind of business we're in, our circle of friends becomes smaller. I can count on the fingers of one hand the people I would call in a dire emergency.   —TRAVIS TRITT, 1995

[Fame is] not something that we sit around and think about, or I don't. But when somebody like Paul McCartney says, "If it wasn't for the Crickets there wouldn't be any Beatles." I say, "Excuse me? I'd like to hear that *again!*"   —JERRY ALLISON, of Buddy Holly's band, the Crickets, 1996

We got to singing and playing one night [on a Caribbean cruise], and the next day one of the people who'd been sitting around listening came up to me and said, "Say, you sure can play that guitar." I thanked him, and then he said, "I'll tell you one thing, though, you ain't no Chet Atkins."   —CHET ATKINS, 1970

ARE YOU SURE HANK DONE IT THIS WAY?

I want you to know, you're the most talented man I've ever fired.

—JIMMY DEAN, to his habitually late lead guitar player, Roy Clark, 1989

I've had to fire myself a couple times.

—SAM BUSH, formerly of New Grass Revival, on making his own business decisions, 1996

I'm a very honest, open person. I think one of the reasons I am a good boss is because you will always know what I'm athinkin'. I won't pout at you or treat you bad. I'll just say, "Hey, Joe, there's somethin' that's really been buggin' the shit outa me." Anybody that works with me will tell you that.   —DOLLY PARTON, 1993

It's important to be able to carry a guitar case in one hand and a briefcase in the other.   —TRAVIS TRITT

I'm out there for the joy of playing music in front of people. I shouldn't bring my business out there with me. The stage is the place for the artist, not the businessman. That's what writes the next record. That's what creates the next expression. And if your writing suffers, your soul suffers.   —HAL KETCHUM, 1995

You should never, ever give up your artistic integrity, but I think you should never, ever stop trying to succeed at the hard-core mainstream with it.   —MARTY STUART, 1995

Commercial failure has given me the freedom to experiment . . . a lot.   —ROSANNE CASH, 1996

If you've had some hit records, and all of a sudden you picture yourself a big businessman, you can go down the tube right quick. There's an old saying, "A good executive is one who can successfully pick people who can handle things for him."

—CONWAY TWITTY (1933–1993)

It's called the old-school mentality . . . and it is what has gotten so many country music artists in trouble. It's the theory you have to cram everything into a couple of years because the career might not last any longer than that. —WYNONNA JUDD, 1996

You have to want it bad. You have to be persistent. If you're afraid of competition, you should probably go home.

—HOLLY DUNN, on how to make it in the music business, 1995

Hell, if you don't play guitar or sing any better than I do, you better have a lot of perseverance.

—KIX BROOKS, of Brooks & Dunn, 1994

> # THOSE WHO CAN COMPETE, DO. THOSE WHO CAN'T, BITCH.
> —KENNY ROGERS, 1996

I've never seen a horse win a race that took the time to turn around and see where his competition was. Because once he makes that move to turn and see what everybody else is doing, that split second, someone is past him.

—SCOTT HENDRICK, president and CEO of Capitol Records in Nashville, 1996

[Dottie West] didn't come in [the recording studio] with a baby, she didn't come in cryin' on my shoulder. She come and said, "I'm a singer and I want to sing." She had the drive, personality, and will power. —TOMMY HILL, record producer, 1996

You know, this is show business. It's not a religion. It's only country music, and it's only show business. People shouldn't take it too seriously. Do what I did when I got into it—have a good time. Just don't try to have as much fun as I did. —TOM T. HALL, 1993

I'm just a hippie. I think the reason I got into show business was I thought it would be the easiest way to buy a farm.
—LACY J. DALTON, 1993

We didn't have a clue [about the business], we didn't know anybody and we had no idea how to get in. But we were so naive we didn't even know we didn't have a clue. —JOHN WIGGINS, 1994

[Waylon Jennings] asked me for some friendly advice on moving to Nashville, giving up a good job with a higher-than-average income to dig for some gold on Nashville's 16th Avenue concrete. Naturally, I told him to stay where he was. Fortunately, he didn't listen.
—WILLIE NELSON, 1978

What kept me in the business was that if I did anything else, I didn't know if I could even live. [Music] and pickin' cotton are about all I know how to do. And they got cotton-pickin' machines now. So I'm in trouble if I have to go back to that.
—WAYLON JENNINGS, 1984

[Show business] sure beats the heck out of working in a beauty shop and picking cotton. —TAMMY WYNETTE, 1996

When I leave this business, it will be with my hands folded, lying in a box. —PORTER WAGONER

I'm a student of this business. This is what I want to do. There's not any other business I want to go into. So if this is what I'm going to be doing for the rest of my life, and I fully intend this or some part of this, then I might as well jump in with both feet.
—TIM McGRAW, 1996

There was one time in '87 when I wanted to say, "Done." I tried everything. I told my mom, "I quit." She let me go through my whole speech and said, "Right. What're you going to do?" I thought about it and said, "I'd better get back to work."

—MARTY STUART, 1994

That's what show business is made of, disappointments. And it's through those disappointments that you grow. As somebody said, "If show business was easy, everybody'd be doing it."

—MINNIE PEARL (1912–1996), 1988

Show business was my life until I started trying to make a living at it.

—JEANNIE SEELY

This business is funny. You go from nothingness, from being absolutely idle when you've signed your deal and you're just waiting for the record to come out, to full steam ahead. Just rockin' and rollin' and slammin'.

—TOBY KEITH, 1994

The only thing I live my life for is to be home and to do my little show, one-hour, hour-and-a-half show, out on the road. Home and the show; the rest I just put up with.

—JOHN MICHAEL MONTGOMERY, 1996

If the girls don't sing, the boys don't eat.

—NAOMI JUDD, on making the payroll, 1993

I poor-boyed it for 21 years. I don't feel like some kind of money-making machine. That's not what I'm in this business for. Man, I just love what I'm doin' and if them other guys don't, let 'em get out.

—SAMMY KERSHAW, 1993

Don't tell anybody, but this is fun. This is the job we've both dreamed about having our whole lives. Sometimes we'll just break down and say to each other, "You know what, you can't believe the amount of fun I'm having!" We don't even want the public to know—they'd hate us, man! And to get paid for it, too! Unbelievable. —RONNIE DUNN, of Brooks & Dunn, 1995

I sat in on the first half of contract negotiations, and spent the rest of it sick. I just never seen numbers like that. —GARTH BROOKS, 1995

For years we didn't know how to read our [financial] statements and we didn't know enough to hire our own lawyers to negotiate our contracts. The record companies and the middlemen would tell us, "You don't need a lawyer. You're a good ole country boy, and I'm a good ole country boy. We're just good, plain, honest folks. . . . Sign this contract and let's go have a beer, pal." Waylon [Jennings] to this day says when somebody calls him "pal" it makes him paranoid. —WILLIE NELSON, 1988

They say that I beat the system. I didn't do that. The system was after my ass—it don't know when to quit. There's nothing human about it. It runs itself. —WAYLON JENNINGS, 1984

I don't know if I'd go into show business again. It's an unnatural life. And it's cut-throat. People are always doin' and asayin' ugly things. —LORETTA LYNN

This business is like walking through a swamp with 90 percent quicksand. —CONWAY TWITTY (1933–1993)

THE MUSIC BUSINESS IS STRICTLY BUSINESS.

—KENNY ROGERS

Sometimes it's like you're a big pie settin' on the table, and everybody runs up and gets their piece of you. When it's over, the plate's empty. —LORETTA LYNN

My attitude is that I've always known there are bad people in this world, and I for some reason believed I was safe from that; of course, now I have hard evidence that I'm just like everyone else. If you put your blind faith in someone, you may have grave consequences.   —CLINT BLACK, on bad management, 1995

We was driving along in a pickup truck, and [Tennessee Ernie Ford] turns to me and says, "You ever managed anybody before?" I said, "No. Just myself." And he said, "Well, I never been managed, so why don't we start off even?" We shook hands in a pick-up truck. Never had a written contract of any kind. Never.

—CLIFFIE STONE, Tennessee Ernie Ford's first manager, 1996

Kenny and I were talking about careers. And I explained, "Careers are like small airplanes. If you get up to a certain height and, even if you turn the engine off, you glide for a long time. Kenny, you won't hit the ground in your own lifetime." There was a big, long silence, and he said, "Ken, I think I'm planning to live a lot longer than you think."   —KEN KRAGEN, Kenny Rogers's manager, 1996

I almost broke up with my manager over [changing my name]. It was just horrible for me. It was part of that "I'll go to Nashville, and they'll give me some sickening name, and make me bleach my hair, and give me a boob job, and make me lose twenty pounds." Then I'd be just like everything else—a homogenized version of me.

—LACY J. DALTON, 1988

OUR PRODUCER TOLD US WE WE'RE EITHER GONNA BE [CALLED] SHENAN-DOAH OR THE RHYTHM RANGERS. NOW WHICH ONE WOULD YOU HAVE PICKED?

—MARTY RAYBON, of Shenandoah, 1995

Patsy should have been a wealthy woman from the way everything was going as a result of "Walkin' After Midnight." Had she been signed directly to Decca, Patsy wouldn't have a financial worry in the world. It was a disgrace the way she was taken advantage of by [Bill] McCall. He had her coming and going.

—CHARLIE DICK, Patsy Cline's husband, on her first producer, Bill McCall, 1993

No matter what I'd do, I couldn't please [Patsy Cline]. She'd start in, "Owen, I want to do it this way." And I'd say no. . . . She was always trying to get her way. . . . I kidded her that she was responsible for my first gray hairs. . . . I soon discovered I had to place myself firmly in control or she'd take right over.

—OWEN BRADLEY, producer, 1993

[Owen Bradley would] station himself between us and Patsy and just go to town laying it off on her. And she'd lay it right back. "Young lady, you're gonna do this my way," Bradley would say. "Oh, no, I'm not," she'd protest. "Don't you forget I'm the one driving this wagon!" he'd say. And she'd yell back, "Don't you forget who's your best passenger!"

—GORDON STOKER, of the Jordanaires, on recording with Patsy Cline and her producer, Owen Bradley, 1993

I don't see making a record as a struggle between the artist and the producer. I want the artist to win, because if the artist wins, everybody wins. The most important thing is only signing acts you believe in. You don't just look at their music, you also look at what they're about. You want to see their determination, how hard they'll fight for their music and their career. You almost become a detective and see if there are any skeletons in their closet. It's like a marriage, and nobody likes to go through divorces.

—TONY BROWN, president MCA Records in Nashville, 1996

[Executives] like [artists] that are humble and have an "aw, shucks" kind of attitude toward the business. I worked a lot of rough places and worked on my music and got fired from a lot of jobs and ate

Vienna sausage sandwiches for six months at a time 'cause that's all you could afford. I did that for a lot of years, and to sit back and say, "Well golly gosh, I'm just so glad that I've been given this opportunity and I really don't deserve this" would be a lie.

—TRAVIS TRITT, 1995

There used to be a guy with RCA that would come in and say, "You just be quiet, and we will take care of this. We know what we are doing. . . ." Now where is that coming from—he knows what he is doing about *my* music? Telling me what to release, and then he sits there and pats his foot to the wrong beat. And he whistled with a Yankee accent.   —WAYLON JENNINGS, 1979

I draw from being around people who are better [than me]. It is amazing to me that some [producers] in this business don't even know when a musician or an artist crosses the line, going from being good or great to beyond being great. Maybe the reason I can spot it was because I was never excellent myself. I know the difference.

—TONY BROWN, president of MCA Records in Nashville, 1996

The industry is uncomfortable with intelligent artists.

—TRAVIS TRITT, 1994

If I'm good right now, it's because of experience, not because I'm particularly bright.   —LUKE LEWIS, president of Mercury Records, 1996

It's at least a million per record that like what we do. So no matter how many walls or mountains you face within the industry, tryin' to get this recognition or that recognition, the bottom line is that they can't ever take that platinum record away from you.

—COLLIN RAYE, 1995

Man, this whole [music business] is one big insecurity blanket. You're only as good as your next record. If it's a hit, you feel a rush and get a bit of attention. If it's not, though, it's the worst feeling in the world, especially if you wrote the song.

—MARK COLLIE, 1994

If I hear "demographics" one more time, I'm gonna puke right in their faces.   —JOHNNY CASH, his opinion of his record label, 1992

The country fan and the country artist are at the mercy of an industry concerned only with quick money. . . . "Broadening" the appeal simply means destroying its true identity.

—RALPH COMPTON, 1993

I'll make records. Whether the mainstream country wants to play 'em, I don't know. . . . I still love country music, but the mainstream is just so squeaky-clean right now. I think people need to get a little dirty and color outside the lines a bit.

—EMMYLOU HARRIS, 1996

Sure, the country singers want to be pop. It's the difference between selling 70,000 singles and selling 500,000 singles. Money does it every time.

—BILL WILLIAMS, former Country Music Association president, 1970

MASS MARKETING HAS DONE MORE TO KILL PASSION IN ART THAN ANYTHING.

—K. T. OSLIN, 1993

Television feeds off people like Conway Twitty or Loretta Lynn or Mac Davis—whoever. You can burn yourself out right quick that way. They'll use you up, and they don't care, 'cause there are others standin' in line right behind you. I refuse to let them feed on me.

—CONWAY TWITTY (1933–1993)

We're currently—have been for the last couple years, at least—in a real pop atmosphere in country. And I'm not really crazy about it.

That's my Okie country side. I'd like to go deep sometimes, in terms of lyric content. But you can literally be stopped by the market.

—RONNIE DUNN, of Brooks & Dunn, 1994

Randy Travis would be the first one to tell you, less than four years ago he was the Garth Brooks of our age now. During that time period, he could not lose. Now he's virtually ignored by every major award show in the country. One day you're in, the next day you're out.

—TRAVIS TRITT, 1993

I was in a recording studio . . . and someone from Randy Travis's record company walks in. I asked him what was going on, and he said, "Nothing, we're just looking for the new Randy Travis." I said, "What's wrong with the one you got?"

—JOHNNY CASH, 1994

> # I LOOKED UP, AND THE BUZZARDS WERE CIRCLING MY CAREER.
> —ROGER MILLER (1936–1992)

TURN YOUR RADIO ON

People talk about how when you [first] hear one of your songs on the radio, you pull by the side of the road and you just have to listen, you can't drive. Luckily, I was at a stoplight. —JOHN TIRRO, 1996

When I found myself singing over the radio, I didn't think life got much better than that. —WILLIE NELSON, 1980

FM radio has hurt traditional country music. . . . "Seven in a row," I mean, you play seven in a row of the New Country, and you don't know who's coming up. All these people were singing: the Nitty Gritty Dirt Band, and Julio and Willie. . . . They might play a George Strait song next, and then they'll play Earl Thomas Conley and Reba McEntire, and then they might play Olivia Newton-John, who *hates* country music. [People are] so tired of "seven in a row" that they want to puke. —MEL TILLIS, 1988

Country music hasn't been on the radio for years.

—DALE WATSON, singer-songwriter, on the decline of true country music, 1995

I don't listen to a lot of country radio because I don't hear enough songs that sound country to me. That's my privilege—it's my radio. —TOM T. HALL, 1996

What's happening with country radio? Is this one-size-fits-all approach strangling country music? Should [a] handful of consultants be able to decide what country music sounds like? Should songwriters have to blunt their creativity trying to come up with

~93

something that will fit the cookie cutter? Should artists be restricted by image or age or anything else except the quality and acceptance of their music? God bless country music.   —CHARLIE DANIELS, 1996

Say you came from New York and you never had heard country music, but when you did finally listen to it there were some things you liked. I mean, most of it was just too damned corny and scratchy for you, but there were certain songs you liked because they were smoother. So then they started modernizing it more because the disc jockeys began to get more requests whenever something came out that was a little smoother. . . . They finally combined the two, but still kept that simple story line that to me is country music: the pathos, the miseries, the happiness, life itself, that's what it's all about. And they could get that in there and still they wouldn't have to be so damned nasal, whiny, and scratchy and corny. . . . It's just good business, to get the best of both worlds.

—JACK STRAPP, of Tree Publishing, 1970

Country music is still all about radio. There's 2,800 radio stations out there that play country music. That's still where it's at.

—ALLEN BUTLER, president of Sony Music in Nashville, 1996

What's happened is they've let a good bit of mediocrity slip into our business, where at one time only veterans and great ones stood.

—JOHN ANDERSON, on the decline of country radio, 1993

We think artists and producers are indulgent and not disciplined in many cases when they produce songs that are over four minutes.

—DENE HALLAM, program director at KKBQ-AM and
FM in Houston, on playing long singles on the air, 1996

So what if my song is four minutes, 25 seconds? Here's my soul, and I'm sorry if it doesn't fit into your time frame.

—WYNONNA JUDD, 1996

"El Paso" is the classic, greatest song ever written. You can't edit "El Paso" for radio, you can't say, "We'll cut it down to three minutes." . . . If you cut one line, the story collapses. It's a perfectly written song. —GAIL DAVIES, 1996

I can't get played on the radio no more. I've had some good songs I don't think got a full treatment in America. I think it's unfair to the public. —MERLE HAGGARD, 1995

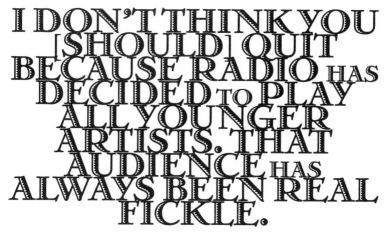

I DON'T THINK YOU [SHOULD] QUIT BECAUSE RADIO HAS DECIDED TO PLAY ALL YOUNGER ARTISTS. THAT AUDIENCE HAS ALWAYS BEEN REAL FICKLE.

—PAUL OVERSTREET, 1996

Country radio has changed enormously, dramatically, just since I had "Honky-Tonk Man" as a hit. It's become more like pop, which is a positive and a negative, a double-edged sword there. It's much more prone to disposing of artists, such a fickle climate.

—DWIGHT YOAKAM, 1996

Radio plays music to sell advertising. It's a business, and . . . radio owners are always looking at the bottom line. They're not interested in my career. They're interested in money and ratings. What can we sell this week? —HELEN DARLING, 1996

One day I woke up and I never heard another George Jones or Merle Haggard tune on the radio. . . . It was like the owners of the stations got together and said, "Hey, if they're not under 35 and don't look like an eight-by-ten glossy, we don't want them." [Radio] is the only section of the music industry that has cut the throats of its elders, especially those who still have a hell of a lot to contribute.

—JOHNNY PAYCHECK, 1996

I worry about the future of a country music community that has no respect for its history. There has never been a time when country radio was so disrespectful of its elders. I'm saddened.

—GEORGE JONES, 1996

Whoever says radio is guilty of age discrimination is just a bunch of crying, whining crybabies, and it's a bunch of sour grapes.

—DENE HALLAM, program director at KKBQ-AM and FM in Houston, 1996

N othing written about me has told it right.

—JOHNNY CASH, 1996

When you're a public figure, everything you do is fair game for . . . "reinterpretation."

—REBA McENTIRE, 1996

They'll take 14 different pictures of you, but publish the one where you're scratching your lip, and it looks like you're pickin' your nose.

—CLINT BLACK, on the tabloids, 1993

I DON'T HAVE ANYTHING TO HIDE . . . OTHER THAN BEING A PSYCHOPATHIC AX MURDERER.

—JOE DIFFIE, on his name being smeared all over the tabloids, 1995

The National Enquirer. And you know what's even funnier than that? I buy it every week, and read it. And *love* to read it! Until I'm in it. And then I'm furious.

—TAMMY WYNETTE, on what makes her angry, 1988

I found [Billy Ray Cyrus] to be a thoroughly personable young man, a perfectly nice person. It made me feel like if I have to read one more Billy Ray Cyrus–bashing article, I'm gonna puke! It's like this guy automatically became a target because he became that successful that quick with a song which—let's face it—is not the most profound thing to hit the airwaves. But why target the guy? Why not target the million people who bought the album?

—MARY CHAPIN CARPENTER, 1993

When the tabloids write stuff about me, I kinda roll with it. [My mother] gets mad and sulks.   —BILLY RAY CYRUS, 1993

You really did it this time, brother! You couldn't have opened a bigger can of worms than if you said Roy Acuff was gay!

—MARTY STUART, to Travis Tritt, after Tritt's comment that Cyrus was turning country music into an "ass wigglin' " contest, 1994

[The press] took [my comment on Billy Ray Cyrus] and turned it against me to sell newspapers. . . . I was asked a question, and I answered it honestly. As a result, I got a tremendous cold shoulder. If that's the attitude I'm going to get for being honest, then to hell with it. I'll pull out. I'll play my concerts, I'll do what I'm supposed to do, but I'll back away from the media in general.

—TRAVIS TRITT, 1994

[Bad press] does roll off of me, because there's nothing you can do about it, first of all. And the public has a right to know, and they definitely have an inquiring mind.   —DOLLY PARTON, 1993

Those stories are written by heartless people who have no careers, other than ruining other people's lives. They've ruined more relationships than they know. . . . It pisses me off! They don't know what goes on behind closed doors.   —LORRIE MORGAN, 1994

THOSE PEOPLE ARE MORE LIKE STALKERS THAN REPORTERS.

—DOLLY PARTON, on tabloid reporters, 1993

Do all the positive things in the world, and the one negative thing you do will stand out and be talked about.

—TRAVIS TRITT, 1994

[The bad press] sustained me and kept my name out there when there weren't any hit records. You know what they say, "As long as they spell my name right."

—TANYA TUCKER, 1993

They've always called me the tabloid queen, and I guess I've gotten some kind of pride in just being the queen of anything! I just want to be the queen.

—DOLLY PARTON, 1993

[The press] always go into that macho stuff when they write about me. They make it sound like my main interest in life is tearing things apart. They forget I'm a musician. That's all I've ever been.

—WAYLON JENNINGS, 1979

You get some reporters, and they just want to belabor the point, and elaborate on it until you've chewed your cabbage twice, you know? And I just say, "I'm Charley Pride, the man. American."

—CHARLEY PRIDE, on the media's obsession with his being an African-American country singer, 1988

I'm not witty. It doesn't come easy to talk [to interviewers]. It's sometimes hard to go along with the obligations that go along with getting your music heard. I want to talk about the songs, but I don't want everybody to know that I got "slam-dunked" or went through "unscheduled open-heart surgery."

—MARY CHAPIN CARPENTER, 1993

It amuses me, the people who set themselves up as critics. . . . What do they know? They may have the power to pull down their pants and shit all over you. [But] being true to the heart of your own self puts you way ahead of the game no matter who thinks they're keeping score.

—WILLIE NELSON, 1988

I like hearing good reviews, but bad reviews don't surprise me. Sometimes you feel like you're fooling half the people who like you.

—TIM McGRAW, 1996

. . . NO MORE THAN A BAREFOOT, BRALESS, PLEASANT-SOUNDING COUNTRY SINGER.

—A *Rolling Stone* review of newcomer Linda Ronstadt

THE ARTISTIC
TEMPERAMENT

I've learned that I've hurt a lot of people while enjoyin' my success, and I've hurt a lot of people in marriage, I've hurt a lot of people just standin' by me—close friends. . . . You hurt kinfolk. You're just havin' a good time, and you don't pay attention to who you hurt, and nothin' is of any importance except yourself. —GEORGE JONES, 1988

I think when people see themselves as the stars that other people do, it's pretty much all over. —REBA McENTIRE, 1993

I think people expect Ronnie [Dunn] and me to be swinging from the chandeliers when they meet us after a show. I think sometimes the fans are surprised that we just stand there and talk to 'em like *normal people.* —KIX BROOKS, of Brooks & Dunn, 1993

My fans and writers are always makin' a big deal about me actin' natural, right from the country. That's because I come from Butcher Holler, and I ain't never forgot it. —LORETTA LYNN, 1976

I don't pay attention to that. I feel honored with what those words are supposed to mean, but I'm just a down-to-earth ol' country boy, and I love to sing. —GEORGE JONES, on being called a legend, 1988

It's really a compliment, in a way. But it sure makes you sound old. —WILLIE NELSON, on being called a legend, 1988

I've been able to make a living playing music, doing what I want to do. And at the same time create some sort of reputation that people admire . . . and I have no idea how I did that. I really don't know how that came about.　　　　　　　—MERLE HAGGARD, 1996

Yeah, I can see the industry and the people being through with me. If I had the talent of Johnny Cash or Merle Haggard, sure. But I'm not those guys. Those guys are legends, and those guys know how to be legends.　　　　　　　—GARTH BROOKS, 1994

I'm shy, I really am. And I don't know what to say when somebody says they like my records. Except "Thank you." If I ain't got no rocks to kick and say, "Aw, shit," I'm in trouble.
　　　　　　　—WAYLON JENNINGS, 1985

All I do is, I do the best I can do. I do what I know how to do. I'm not out there to change the world. I just do what I do and hope somebody appreciates it.　　　　　　　—MARK CHESNUTT, 1995

I believe what I do best is go out there, tell stories, and sing out of tune. I think I'm pretty good at that after all these years.
　　　　　　　—JOHN PRINE, 1995

[Ernest Tubb] wasn't that great a singer, he'd be the first to tell you. In fact, he said many times, the reason he was successful and as big as he was, is because any drunk could go up to the jukebox, play one of his records, and say, "Hell, I can sing *that* good!" And then they'd play it again.　　　　　　—JUSTIN TUBB, Ernest Tubb's son, 1996

> ## I BELIEVE THAT EVERYBODY CAN LEARN TO PLAY THE PIANO. IT'S NOTHIN'; IT'S NOTHIN' GREAT. IT'S JUST THE WAY *I* DO IT THAT'S GREAT.
> —JASON D. WILLIAMS, singer and piano man, 1996

I won't say anything about my musical ability. That's a matter of taste, isn't it? What I *do* want people to say is that I was stubborn and opinionated in everything else, from business to politics. Because if you aren't, you got no vision, and who needs you?

—ROY ACUFF (1903–1992)

I'm gonna do this my way. I'm gonna do it like I want to do it. If you don't like it, then kiss my ass and get out of the way.

—DWIGHT YOAKAM, 1994

I don't play games. I don't do nothin' but sing. I'm gonna go out there and do my thing . . . and you can like it or you can not like it. I really couldn't care less, because I'm happy at *this* one time.

—SHELBY LYNNE, 1993

People used to ask me when Jessi had her first big pop hit, "How does it feel when she has a pop hit right out of the shoot and you don't have one?" "Well," I says, "being a goddamn legend, I don't really give a damn."

—WAYLON JENNINGS, on the success of his wife, Jessi Colter, 1980

There are people that set trends, that are in front of the curve. I want to be in front of the curve. I don't know what the curve is, but I want to be in front of it.

—MARC ALAN BARNETT, 1996

What happens is that you get caught up in what everybody else is doing and comparing yourself, and that's when you're in trouble.

—KATHY MATTEA, on the difficulty of maintaining individuality in the country music business, 1995

I've been very guilty of being just totally high on myself. There's an old quote, and I can't remember who said this, but there are periods in your life where you assume that there are two types of people . . . me and those who are not me. And you've got to be careful of that. You've got to stay real.

—HAL KETCHUM, 1996

I came here thinking that country music needed me. I didn't dream there would be a million other people thinking the same thing.

—GARTH BROOKS, 1993

I want to take charge. I'm always greedy. I want to do more. I've never been content with my life. . . . I'm very competitive, very ambitious. Who don't like to win? You show me a person who don't like to win.

—REBA McENTIRE

There's a guy I'd love to be, and the guy I am. I'm somewhere in between.

—MERLE HAGGARD, 1994

I'm a "take me as I am" person, and all the rest is water under the bridge. What I try to do is live with myself and please me. If I can't do that, I can't please anybody else or live with anybody else.

—GLEN CAMPBELL, 1980

It always seems like I am standing outside of me watching the whole thing go down, whatever I'm doing.

—GARTH BROOKS, 1994

I'm the motherfucker who has to live with David Allan Coe for the rest of his life.

—DAVID ALLAN COE, 1988

I'm so damned unlucky, if I died and got reincarnated, I'd probably come back as myself.

—FREDDY FENDER

Hell, how could [the public] have liked me? I didn't like me. I had a serious case of cranial rectumitis.

—LARRY GATLIN, 1993

I never was ashamed of not havin' an education. There was nothin' I could do about. If there'da been somethin' I coulda done about it, then I'da been ashamed.

—LORETTA LYNN, 1993

I'm not offended by all the dumb-blonde jokes because I know that I'm not dumb. I also know that I'm not blonde.

—DOLLY PARTON, 1993

I been a "bubba" forever. I been this [round] shape my whole life. I never changed shapes, I just got bigger. If you shaved my head, pulled out all my teeth, and put me in a diaper, I would look like I was 18 months old right now. —T. BUBBA BECHTOL, comic, 1995

Mama made me be in a beauty contest. And I didn't think that the people would laugh at me, but they did. They fell out. One of the best laughs I've ever gotten. . . . That was one of the times I realized that some of us are not suppose to play it straight.

—MINNIE PEARL (1912–1996), 1988

My neck's too long, my nose has a lump in it, and I have to use mustache wax on my eyebrows to keep 'em in place. They fall down. I like my lips. I'm satisfied with my eyes. My boobs are too saggy, and the kids call me "weenie butt." —TAMMY WYNETTE, 1988

WELL, I AM THE GOOFIEST WOMAN IN COUNTRY MUSIC, A TITLE I WEAR PROUDLY.

—NAOMI JUDD, 1994

When you look like me, you can't take a bad picture, because no matter what angle you get, it's going to look like it's going to look. . . . It's because I'm ugly. . . . You can't make me look pretty or different. —MARK COLLIE, 1994

If I were a young man, I'd be just as ugly as I am now. And there are some of these young fellas [in the country music industry] as ugly as homemade soap! —BILLY JOE SHAVER, 1993

I'd rather be like Schwarzenegger—perfect teeth, perfect body, full head of hair. —GARTH BROOKS, 1994

All of us are constantly in comparison to the perfect model. Look at yourself in the mirror and say, well, I'm okay. —K. D. LANG, 1993

I guess it's like my daddy said: "You shouldn't try to cram 50 pounds of mud into a five-pound sack."

—DOLLY PARTON, after her bosom burst from its bodice at a Country Music Association Awards show

When I walked onstage [at the 1993 Country Music Association Awards], I heard [the audience gasp]. I didn't dare look down. . . . I got more press from that red dress than if I'd won Entertainer of the Year. —REBA McENTIRE, on the reaction to her low-cut gown, 1996

Female stars are vigorously hair-sprayed and overcoiffed and are expected to keep their legs crossed until marriage (however, multiple marriages are looked upon favorably—they mean she's suffered), to require frequent hospitalization for "exhaustion," to be anti-abortion, and not to publicly endorse the Equal Rights Amendment. Male stars are tough, leathery, and pink-skinned and are encouraged to be obsessed with railroads, guns, prison, and mistreated Indians. Female stars are forgiven for not knowing how to dress properly. Male stars are forgiven for obesity, adultery, wife-beating, and alcoholism. Stars of both sexes also are expected to espouse the virtues of Mom, the flag, and pecan pie; wear their battle scars in public (as long as it's good publicity); and always preface each award acceptance speech by thanking Him, the Man upstairs, or some other such acceptable euphemism for God.

—RANDALL RIESE, *Nashville Babylon*, 1988

> ## IT TAKES A LOT OF MONEY TO MAKE ME LOOK THIS CHEAP.
> —DOLLY PARTON, 1993

What made Patsy [Cline] stand out was the way she dressed. The things she wore—tight-fitting dresses, dangly earrings, and those spike heels—were the type a loose woman'd wear. And the way she painted her lips red! A lot of men and women thought she was sexy.

—JOSEPH SHREWBRIDGE, fiddle player, 1993

Patsy [Cline] was a sexy girl. She had a full figure. Patsy wasn't overweight, but a big girl. She went in for a little shorter dresses than most of the girls. Her wardrobe had a lot to do with her being known as a sex symbol. Patsy wore her clothes tight around the hips. She liked sequins and gold and silver lamé. And she could wear 'em. And high-heeled shoes. It kind of went with her. It was the package.

—MINNIE PEARL (1912–1996)

I don't move around a hell of a lot, maybe wiggle my legs every now and then. Changin' my clothes 50 times in a set; I don't believe in that crap. People come to hear you sing. They don't give a damn what clothes you can afford to wear.

—GEORGE JONES, 1995

The fans deserve to see something special, to feel like you wore something special for them. It's part of the ticket price, part of the show.

—JEANNIE SEELY, 1996

Someone who's performing should not look like she just got out of the audience and walked onstage.

—BARBARA MANDRELL, 1996

It's become an identifying mark to wear fancy clothes on stage. Some guys dress down; I dress up.

—BILLY WALKER, 1996

When I first put my band together, I started calling guys in Porter Wagoner's old band asking if they had any old Nudie [designer Paul "Nudie" Cohen] suits. . . . I bought their old hillbilly costumes because no one was wearing them. Everyone thought we were cowpunks, but it was just a way of dressing a band at an affordable price.

—MARTY STUART, on the traditional rhinestone cowboy outfits, 1996

I still have a wardrobe of gaudy costumes, but it's not often I wear them. If I play a rodeo, maybe I'll whip on a rhinestone suit. The rhinestones were always kind of a nuisance anyway, because they scratched up the guitars. Country has moved uptown a lot. The day of the Cadillac cowboy is gone.

—HANK WILLIAMS, JR., 1996

People see me like this when I'm in the supermarket buying milk or something, and sometimes they'll sort of sidle up to me real slyly and say, "Traveling incognito, hmm?" I just tell 'em, "No, this is me. I always dress this way!"

—MARY CHAPIN CARPENTER, on her informal style, 1995

Lots of women buy just as many wigs and makeup things as I do. . . . *THEY* just don't wear them all at the same time.

—DOLLY PARTON

We've given up the big hair and fluffy dresses, and we're influenced by all the European designers.   —TANYA TUCKER, 1996

I think it's very important for anybody in the limelight, whether it be a hair transplant, a boob job, a face lift, nose changed, eyes—whatever. I would do it. Because I think a show is exactly what it says—a show.   —TAMMY WYNETTE, on plastic surgery, 1988

Yes, I've had several little things done . . . and several big ones!

—DOLLY PARTON, on plastic surgery, 1996

MY WIFE WON'T LET ME.

—ALAN JACKSON, on shaving his mustache and cutting his trademark hair, 1995

This business is real image-oriented. You gotta compete with the Clint Blacks and Alan Jacksons, and those are some real handsome guys. So you got to look as best you can. I'd hate to screw up a career being overweight.   —JOE DIFFIE, 1993

Image is something added on to you.   —JERRY JEFF WALKER, 1994

You can play with your image all day long, back and forth, outlaw, rebel, romantic, balladeer, whatever you want to do, but if you don't have good songs, it's all going to amount to, as Charlie Daniels once said, "a nickel's worth of warm piss."

—TRAVIS TRITT, 1994

Anybody who's afraid to tamper with his image has a limited time in this business. Music is ever-changing and you have to go with it.

—KENNY ROGERS, 1993

I'm not a cowboy. I'm not a biker. I don't have a particular image. Most of the people who have huge careers have some kind of image they're trying to project. I never came up with one that made any sense, so my focus has always been on the music and what it means to the fans.

—COLLIN RAYE, 1996

It doesn't matter to a real music fan whether the guy has on a hat or not. The real talents, when it gets an audience, will show through.

—WILLIE NELSON, 1994

Vince Gill once said that he was gonna buy a cowboy hat as a career move.

—TOM WOPAT, actor, 1996

[Marty Brown] doesn't have to have the hat to play. It's a ratty hat, all battered from the road. More a hobo's hat than a cowboy hat. Not the kind of hat George Strait would even handle, much less wear. Paid $80 bucks for it when he was only making $90 a week working in a grocery store. Blocked it himself with the help of steam from a teakettle, his grocery store tie and hair spray. But understand this: It's not like it's a hat he has to have to get out there on stage, you know, like a good luck charm or something like that. It's a hat, see, that's part of him.

—MICHAEL BANE, journalist, 1993

The significance of the price tag is that, in the country, where I was raised, if you got anything new (most of the time you wore hand-me-downs from your sisters), but if you got anything new, you wanted to wear it out of the store.

—MINNIE PEARL (1912–1996), explaining the price tag that hung from her signature straw hat

It's a great compliment when they drop the labels off of you. Labels are just to tell people where you're at, and if they can't listen to you and know where you're at, then you're in trouble anyway.

—WAYLON JENNINGS, 1975

I play a lot of shows where it's an older crowd, and you don't want to alienate those people. Then you've got your new people who are hungry and rumblin' and maybe would love somebody with a little more kick-butt image. The thing is I think it's easiest to just dispense with image and be yourself.

—PAM TILLIS, 1993

Often in country music these days, you're dealing with people who are trying to keep their real selves secret—it's media manipulation, image control; managers and record companies actually have their "artists" coached in how to do it. It's a tonic to run into somebody who doesn't care.

—PATRICK CARR, journalist, on interviewing Mark Chesnutt, 1995

> WE'RE NOT SWINGIN' FROM ROPES
> [ONSTAGE] . . . AND I'M NOT NO SEX
> GOD AND DON'T WANT TO BE. I'M JUST
> A SINGER, AND WITH ME IT'S ALL
> MUSIC, IT'S MUSIC AND FUN.
> —MARK CHESNUTT, 1995

We do marketing tests that ask the consumer to associate one word or phrase with various stars. When we hold up a picture of Johnny

Cash, they say, "Black." Kenny Rogers is usually "the Gambler." You know what they say about Willie [Nelson]? The consumer says, "Free spirit."   —BILL BLACKBURN, then president of CBS Records, 1988

[Garth Brooks] has moods like everybody else. In private you'll sometimes see the other side of him. But when he's in public, he'll never let it show.   —MICKEY WEBER, Garth Brooks's road manager, 1994

I think there's definitely something strange, an irony, to me being in [the country music] field. It requires an openness, an accessibility, that kind of goes against my personality.
                                    —MARY CHAPIN CARPENTER, 1993

I'm a real character. I'm exaggerated in every way. I catch your attention with my big wigs and big boobs and my big rear end, too. I want my looks to match what I feel inside, and I want it to be overwhelming.   —DOLLY PARTON, 1993

OUTLAWS &
TROUBLEMAKERS

Them radio people don't want no real outlaws, just somebody that looks like one.

—DAVID ALLAN COE, 1988

I think I got into trouble as a teenager on purpose. I felt the need to experience the things I'd heard about in Jimmie Rodgers's songs. Jesse James was my hero. —MERLE HAGGARD, 1989

When we give honest opinions or talk about things in an honest and open manner, society tends to penalize us for that. I think that's wrong. I was always raised to tell the truth, no matter what. Even if it does get you into trouble from time to time. I think people respect you if you say honestly what you really believe and back it up.

—TRAVIS TRITT, 1993

I don't understand why [the industry] don't want to give me credit for the things that I do. Are they really that intimidated by me? Are they that afraid? There's a voice inside of me that says, "Why do you think they killed Martin Luther King, or Malcolm X?" But I'm sayin', "Yes, but I'm just a musician. I'm just a singer. I'm not a prophet. I'm not a politically minded person." Why are they so afraid of the truth, of the things I say?

—DAVID ALLAN COE, 1988

I don't kiss nobody's butt. —DOLLY PARTON, 1988

I'm the toughest son of a bitch that ever shat out of a mean ass.

—JERRY LEE LEWIS, 1988

You can knock me down, but you better have a big rock to keep me there. —DOTTIE WEST (1932–1991)

I never get tired of people telling me I'm not as big of a pain in the ass as they thought I was going to be. —TRAVIS TRITT, 1994

I'm changin' my image, to one who gives a lesser shit than he used to. —MERLE HAGGARD, 1988

I ALWAYS DO WHAT I'M EXPECTED TO DO. EXCEPT WHEN I DON'T.

—WILLIE NELSON, 1996

Every so often Willie would just stand up and leave the stage, and nobody noticed. He said he reserved the right to just go away. —BILLY JOE SHAVER, on performing with Willie Nelson, 1993

Ninety percent of the people that I've met in this business with a rep for being "hard to deal with or real assholes" turned out to be some of the nicest people I've ever met. —TRAVIS TRITT, 1994

It takes a lot of strain and guts to fight the system. You see, I'm considered outside the system. If I win, they feel like they've lost. . . . I don't want to fight with them. I don't want to argue with them. It's just that I'm very vulnerable in this position. But you also find that vulnerability gives you a lot of strength. —WAYLON JENNINGS, 1975

An outlaw is someone who is outside a working system. In my own work, being an outlaw means that when I sit down to write a song, I don't have any form that I follow. . . . There are really no creative boundaries to what I can do on record. It means a lot of creative freedom. —JESSI COLTER, singer-songwriter and Waylon Jennings's wife, 1993

If you're just talking about musically, I love the term "outlaw," because it set me apart from the pack. The problem is people try to bleed it over in your personal life. They say, "Oh, he's an outlaw, huh? That must mean he's hard to get along with. He's a rebel, a renegade. He'd just as soon smack you as look at you. He's hard to work with." And none of those things could be further from the truth. —TRAVIS TRITT, 1996

Country music is slow to change. The folks in Nashville thought Willie [Nelson] and me were just plain crazy when we turned away from what everyone else was doing. Then when what we did succeeded, suddenly everybody became an outlaw.
—WAYLON JENNINGS, 1996

I think that "outlaw" term was just stuck on anybody who didn't do things the usual Nashville way. —SAMMI SMITH, 1993

> # I DON'T DO ANYTHING HALFWAY.
> # HALFWAY IS HALF-ASSED, AND
> # THAT AIN'T FOR ME.
> —PATSY CLINE (1932–1963)

It was common knowledge that you didn't mess with "the Cline." If you kicked her, she'd kick right back.
—DOTTIE WEST (1932–1991), on Patsy Cline

You couldn't get ahead of Patsy [Cline]. If somebody farted in her direction, she'd raise her ass and fart right back. Didn't make no difference to her who you were. She'd tell you to go screw yourself in a minute. —FARON YOUNG (1932–1996), 1993

I have always believed in doing things my own way. If I have to die by the sword, I want to be holding it before I fall on it.
—TRAVIS TRITT, 1994

It's always hard going up against tradition. . . . But to me, it's worth it. For the bottom line on everything is that the artistic urge has to be handled as carefully as sex. —WAYLON JENNINGS, 1975

There's definitely a country music establishment out there. If you're different, then you're seen as a loose cannon, and they don't like loose cannons. . . . You got so many artists out there who will come in and play the game and shut up and sit back and not rock the boat. They do what they're told, and they fit into the format they're told to fit into. . . . They see what's happened to Waylon Jennings and to Hank Williams, Jr., and some other people, and they don't want that controversy. I've been there, and I'm willing to pay the price to be me. —TRAVIS TRITT, 1994

Roy [Acuff] was the meanest boy that ever lived in Knoxville. He'd rather fight than eat. He'd whupped every policeman in Knoxville, at one time.
—BEECHER "PETE" (BASHFUL BROTHER OSWALD) KIRBY, 1996

I ain't goin' back to prison. Hell, I've gotten used to pussy and different things.
—DAVID ALLAN COE, after serving time for possession of burglary tools in 1974, 1976

[Being arrested for assault] was the worst thing that ever happened to me, and the best thing that ever happened. I can say now that it saved me. Going in, it was just like hitting a brick wall. . . . I knew when I walked into [Chillicothe Correctional Institute in Ohio] that I would redo my life. And I did. —JOHNNY PAYCHECK, 1996

I used to dream I was back in the jail. Just the worst dream I could have. Had it for years.
—MERLE HAGGARD, who did time for burglary, 1995

I just don't think prisons do any good. They put [criminals] in there and just make 'em worse, if they were ever bad in the first place, and then when they let 'em out they're just better at whatever put 'em in there in the first place. —JOHNNY CASH, 1970

TAKE THESE CHAINS ═══
FROM MY HEART

T he richest vein running through [country] music's whole history has been the self-expression of some of the most spectacularly brokenhearted sons of bitches who ever opened their mouths in front of a microphone.

—PATRICK CARR, journalist, 1993

[Martina McBride] can sing been-cheated-on songs, been-dumped-on-and-can't-get-over-him songs and I-need-love-real-bad songs without ever sounding pathetic or victimized.

—KAREN ESSEX, writer, 1996

If there is a "typical" country song, it probably tells a tale of lost and unrequited love.

—DOROTHY HORSTMAN, *Sing Your Heart Out, Country Boy,* 1996

Country music, after all, is the evolution of the lament. The Celtic lament. Some of the most compelling songs are about separation and loss.

—HAL KETCHUM, 1996

I may be an eagle when I fly, but I'm a sparrow when it comes to feelings.

—DOLLY PARTON, 1977

The beauty of dropping to the bottom is that it wipes the slate clean.

—KRIS KRISTOFFERSON, 1977

Solitude is desirable. I've always felt like it's creativity's best friend.

—NAOMI JUDD, 1994

That's all depression is, I think—the highest form of self-pity.

—WAYLON JENNINGS, 1975

He started out with a good understanding of what it was to suffer; life just added salt to the wound.

—JEFF ROVIN, *Country Music Babylon*, on Hank Williams, 1993

His [songs] were all about sadness, you know. Grant Turner asked him one time, "Hank, why do you suppose all your songs are so sad?" He said, "Well, Grant, I suppose you just might call me a sadist." That's so beautiful. Now, that's pure, right there. He didn't know what that meant.

—MEL TILLIS, on Hank Williams, 1988

For me, singing sad songs often has a way of healing a situation. It gets the hurt out in the open, into the light, out of the darkness.

—REBA McENTIRE, 1993

I write about things I know: depression, guilt, despair, failed relationships. Everybody has moments of despair; it's just that I exploit mine.

—MARY CHAPIN CARPENTER

I think it takes a strong person to admit when they've been hurt by somebody, or that they even love somebody that doesn't love them back. I don't think showing that vulnerability makes you a weak person.

—KIM RICHEY, songwriter, 1996

In a relationship, when it's over, but you don't want it to be over, you want to know why. . . . If you can sing that in a song, or play that in a song, it can become somethin' [healing] instead of hurtin'; it's a great release.

—DELBERT McCLINTON, 1996

I'M TRYING TO PUT THE ACHE IN THE MUSIC.

—SUSAN LONGACRE

THE WHISKEY AIN'T
WORKIN' ANYMORE

T he country crowd's pill-popping hey-day was the 1960s. The cocaine craze of the late 1970s coincided with the "outlaw" movement and lasted until the "new sobriety" trend of the 1980's replaced it with "12 step" programs.

—MARY A. BUFWACK AND ROBERT K. OERMANN,
Finding Her Voice: The Saga of Women in Country, 1993

All these producers and executives began coming into Nashville from the Coast in the early–mid-eighties . . . saying, "Hey, we're getting tired of dealing with these artists who come in here and get drunk and raise hell. We're gettin' tired of dealing with this artist who goes out there and smokes pot and blows off his interview." Well, I hate to say it, but some of the greatest artists in the world did exactly that. Some of the greatest sonsabitches who ever walked *did* that. But even at their most screwed up, some of these cats came in and cut some real sincere music, while a lot of the guys who got signed because they were straight and sober and somebody in the company liked 'em, they had to have their records fabricated.

—JOHN ANDERSON, 1993

I think I have all the chemistry to be a full-fledged alcoholic or drug addict; I welcome oblivion like an old friend sometimes.

—KRIS KRISTOFFERSON, 1985

I didn't ever kick the drug habit, and I don't think I ever will. There will always be that gnawing.   —JOHNNY CASH, 1989

You've got to play the clubs; you've got to play the honky-tonks. What I found was that you didn't necessarily have to be *part* of it, just because you are playing around a bunch of drunks. You don't have to become one of them. —TRAVIS TRITT, 1994

I've battled the demons of alcohol. You make your life in a bar five nights, six nights a week, you battle the demons. I'm just glad to say I lived through it. —BILLY RAY CYRUS, 1995

I have cleaned up my playmates and playgrounds. I don't go to nightclubs 'cause I know there are things I'd be around that I don't want to do. —JOHNNY CASH, on staying sober

Booze was always easy to come by. Folks were always wanting to buy me a drink and they'd get mad if I turned them down. They didn't get mad very often. —GEORGE JONES, 1996

You go along and think you're just partyin' a little bit, then one day it's got you and you won't admit it to yourself. Drinkin' about put me under the table. —RICKY VAN SHELTON, 1993

It didn't matter how hard and how difficult it got for me. When I looked at Ricky, I knew that he was suffering even more than me. Even though he's the one causin' the pain.
—BETTY SHELTON, wife of Ricky Van Shelton, on her husband's alcoholism, 1995

Going through rehab, you sit there and hear about other people and their life stories, how unloved they were. . . . I just wanted to have a good time. —TANYA TUCKER, 1993

> YOU'RE LOOKIN' AT A GUY WHO COULD BE DRUNK BY FOUR IN THE AFTERNOON. I'M AN ALCOHOLICS ANONYMOUS MIRACLE AND LUCKY TO BE HERE.
> —MAC DAVIS, 1993

What I do is get up and get my ass to [support] meetings, pretty much every day. I don't know how other people deal with their addiction, but this works for me. I tried every other way in the world to stop, and this worked. This has kept me clean for 16 months, which is the longest I've been clean in my life, and I plan to keep it that way.

—STEVE EARLE, 1996

You do [drugs] off and on for several years recreationally, and then one day you wake up and it's not recreational anymore. It's the key emotional element in your life. And that's fuckin' scary.

—ROSANNE CASH, 1988

Charlie [Dick] was a good ole boy. He did his work but liked to have a good time and enjoyed a drink. He introduced me to more kinds of southern bourbon than I knew existed.

—LAWRENCE VAN GELDER, journalist, on Patsy Cline's husband, 1993

[Ernest Tubb] was a different person when he hit the bottle. He could be very difficult. He would drink when he felt emotional pressures and career pressures building up on him, and would drink rather often. But when he was under the influence, what he loved to do was to point out faults in other people.

—RONNIE PUGH, *The Life and Times of Ernest Tubb*, 1996

[Lefty Frizzell] would sit in a restaurant to eat and the first thing he'd do is look at the right side of the menu. And if a steak was more than a dollar and a half, he'd buy a hamburger. He'd say he'd had hard times and wasn't gonna pay that kind of money for food. But he'd walk out of that restaurant, go right across the street and spend 40 dollars on whiskey.

—CHARLIE WALKER, disc jockey and singer, 1996

When you live with an alcoholic, you become their savior. If you fail with them, then you have failed yourself.

—LUCRECIA WILLIAMS HOOVER, Hank Williams's daughter, 1996

Hank and his cousin would watch where [musicians] would hide [their moonshine]. And these little boys would steal their moonshine, their clear whiskey. And [they'd] go out and drink, at 11 years old. It wasn't really being bad children, it was . . . normal.

—ALICE HAYES, former director of the Hank Williams Museum in Crossville, Tennessee, 1996

Takin' a bottle of Darvon and tryin' to kill yourself and gettin' pumped out is not fun. —HANK WILLIAMS, JR., 1988

I got tired of falling down. You either mature or you die.

—ROGER MILLER (1936–1992), on his drug use

I want to show you my big, bright eyes.

—A clean and sober JOHNNY CASH, to Waylon Jennings after kicking his drug habit, 1993

I freed myself from alcohol and chemical dependency in 1975. Before then, my music was who I was. Now my music is what I do and my family is who I am. —B. J. THOMAS, 1996

I'm not in bad shape for a tequila-drinkin' doper. —WILLIE NELSON

MILLER LITE 4.

—KIX BROOKS, of Brooks & Dunn, on what he studied in college, 1995

I'm Indian; I don't drink. I can drink [one] beer and [think I can] whip the state of Texas! —LORETTA LYNN, 1995

Alcohol makes me do things that I'm not always proud of. . . . The next morning [after a binge] I suffer what the coach Darrell Royal calls the re-re's: the regrets and remorses. I'll sit on the side of the bed and think, oh my God, did I really say that? Oh God, I didn't really tell them that shit, did I? Did I really get into a fighting disposition? Did I really start feeling very amorous at the same time I got too drunk to fuck? Oh God. These are the re-re's.

—WILLIE NELSON, 1988

When you quit drinking, suddenly you're hungry all the time. And your relationships start falling apart because you start facing them instead of numbing them out. I've had to face a lot of things, just not picking up the ole bottle of wine and saying, "Ah, heck with it—I'll just live for today."

—BOBBIE CRYNER, 1996

[Johnny Cash] offered me a double-dot Dexie [speed]. I took it. He'd made me so damned nervous by that time, I really needed it. His hands shook and his arms moved in all directions. I just kept thinkin' about how this skinny dude, who was wilder 'n a guinea, was on his way to becomin' a country legend . . . if he could live that long.

—MERLE HAGGARD, on meeting Cash in the men's room of the Grand Ole Opry, 1988

They had a whole bunch of nice little names for them to dress them up, and they came in all colors. Inside the bottles, which cost only eight or ten dollars for a hundred, came at no extra cost, a demon called Deception. With a couple of those pills in me, I had courage and confidence. My energy was multiplied. If I'd ever been shy before an audience, I wasn't anymore. I was personable, outgoing, energetic—I loved everybody.   —JOHNNY CASH, 1993

I became a thief. I stole pills. I stole car keys. I did everything I could. It hurts you so bad. I mean, you either want to be a little hero and help [the addict] out, or you manipulate things to make excuses for them so they can continue to do what they're doing. There comes a time when you have to learn to deal with it.

—JUNE CARTER CASH, on her husband, Johnny Cash, and his pill addiction, 1993

Yes, I do cocaine, but cocaine isn't a killer drug and neither is alcohol. Cocaine and alcohol are okay, up-front drugs.

—JOHNNY PAYCHECK, 1984

I've been like a window blind: I come up, then I have my problems, then I come back down.

—JOHNNY PAYCHECK, on getting, and staying, clean and sober, 1993

Sex feels good, Jim Beam tastes good, but cocaine will kill your ass.

—HANK WILLIAMS, JR., 1979

Cocaine is an insidious drug. It's like a snake. It's really awful. My God, the time you waste with drugs. Getting 'em, doing 'em, recovering from 'em.

—ROSANNE CASH, 1993

I knew toward the end that I was dying. I just didn't know if there was anything I could do about it. That's what addiction is.

—STEVE EARLE, on his heroin addiction, 1996

> # [SMOKING POT] KEEPS ME FROM KILLIN' PEOPLE.
> —WILLIE NELSON, 1995

Marijuana is like sex. If I don't do it every day, I get a headache.

—WILLIE NELSON, 1988

Yeah, I take pills. Uppers. I can't get anything out of smoking [pot]. I sit and grin and that's about all. I go to sleep and put everyone else to sleep around me.

—WAYLON JENNINGS, 1971

I wasn't in control of things, and I knew it. I *was* smart enough to know when not to drive. . . . It was a mess.

—WAYLON JENNINGS, on his past drug abuse, 1993

[Waylon] would swallow a doorknob if you offered him one.

—CARL PERKINS, 1985

I'm not allowed to drive a car 'cause I might pass out. That makes me mad, because I wrote some of my best songs while drivin' along.

—LORETTA LYNN, on her prescription-drug dependency, 1978

Why would a person go to a cocktail party? My mother told me why people do that. She would occasionally tell my father, "I'm goin' into town this afternoon." If he said, "What do you need in town?" she'd say, "Nothin'. I want to see and be seen." Well, I have no need to see or be seen. When I get drunk, I'm better off in bed.

—TOM T. HALL, 1988

I think most sensible human beings know [smoking pot] is not something you send people to the penitentiary for.

—WILLIE NELSON, 1993

Seems like the police would realize that the dealers of the stuff are not the hillbillies, you know? They arrested me on charges of "distributing," which is just crazy! Making the kind of money I make, why in the hell would I want to be in the cocaine distributing business?

—WAYLON JENNINGS, after his 1977 drug charge, which was later dropped

I went to treatment with no intention of doing anything but getting out of jail.   —STEVE EARLE, on recovering from cocaine addiction, 1995

5

POLITICS & PATRIOTISM

REDNECKS, WHITE SOCKS, AND BLUE RIBBON BEER

As we all know, country music radiates a love of this nation. Patriotism. It's good for Americans to hear it. We come away better having heard it.

—RICHARD NIXON (1913–1995)

I don't know how patriotic I'd be if I was poor and hungry.

—JOHNNY CASH, 1970

[It's] an anthem for a time that had no anthem.

—BILLY RAY CYRUS, on his song about the Vietnam War, "Some Gave All," 1993

I don't think people in [government] now have a clue about foreign policy. You know, it's kind of like when you're playing football. . . . If you go in there trying not to get hurt . . . and there's no game plan to follow, you're gonna get slaughtered. . . . Now, if you send somebody into a war without a laid-out plan, with everybody going off in different directions with the idea of "only shoot when you get shot at," people are going to get hurt!

—WAYLON JENNINGS, 1994

The only good thing that ever came from a war was a song, and that's a hell of a way to get them.   —JOHNNY CASH, 1993

There's no doubt about the fact that country music was diffused throughout the world by [World War II] U.S. military forces. . . . They not only took [country music] with them, but gained new converts with people who, prior to that, had never heard country music before.   —LEROY VAN DYKE, 1996

I've never been in the service, certainly never been in combat or shot at, never come back to a world that didn't give a damn. My first concern was that we have absolute respect for all [Vietnam veterans] involved. They're the ones who paid a price.

—TRAVIS TRITT, on making the video for his hit
"Anymore," 1994

When I was growing up, we didn't give a damn about the government. We didn't pay no attention to it, and we weren't really worried about it. But in the past 20 years the kids have become very aware and concerned about the rights and the wrongs. And for that reason I think we're in pretty good shape.

—WAYLON JENNINGS, 1981

If you don't stand behind the President, get the hell over so I can.

—JOHNNY CASH, 1970

In the '40s . . . Roy Acuff got so mad at a governor for saying he was "disgracing the state by making Nashville the hillbilly capital of the world" that he ran for governor.

—PAUL HEMPHILL, *The Nashville Sound:
Bright Lights and Country Music*

America is a nation that is richer in spirit because of Tennessee Ernie Ford. —RONALD REAGAN, 1984

ANY MAN WHO IS 69 WITHOUT GRAY HAIR MUST KNOW SOMETHING.
—GLEN CAMPBELL, on then President Ronald Reagan, 1980

I'm a conservative. A little bit Democrat and a little bit Republican, but I'm a whole lot Harry Truman!

—WAYLON JENNINGS, 1994

Particularly the urban North has often looked at country music as something connected to Republican Party values or rural values or politically conservative values. But if you look at the stances of so many country songs, it's not partisan.

—BILL IVEY, executive director of the Country
Music Foundation, 1996

Anything that becomes as big as ["Okie from Muskogee"] did has got to have something more than a beer-belly mentality to it. Of course, a lot of people think you have to have a beer-gut mentality to be proud of a particular thing. In other words, you should be ashamed to be proud.

—MERLE HAGGARD, on negative reaction to
his hit "Okie from Muskogee," 1994

We're Americans, we believe in our rights in the Williams household.

—HANK WILLIAMS, JR., on his right to own firearms, 1996

Flag burning? I think about the time June and I went to Viet Nam in 1969 and saw the burning flesh. Whether the war was right or not, a lot of people sacrificed their lives. I cherish all the freedom we have, including the freedom to burn flags. But I also have the freedom to bear arms, and if you burn my flag, I'll shoot you.

—JOHNNY CASH, 1989

A great American takes great pride in what he does, no matter what it is. . . . I meet them every day. I think we're led to think that the majority is an unsatisfied worker who wishes he'd been a lawyer, and that's hogwash.

—AARON TIPPIN, 1996

There is a great tradition of social commentary in country songs. I think it should be encouraged more today than it is. There's a whole tradition of coal-mining songs, such as Tennessee Ernie Ford's "Sixteen Tons," a social commentary if I ever heard one. There's a whole lot of cotton-mill songs, tons of anti-alcohol songs. Other themes include patriotism, labor union songs, some railroad things are social commentary.

—ROBERT K. OERMANN, country music
historian and journalist, 1996

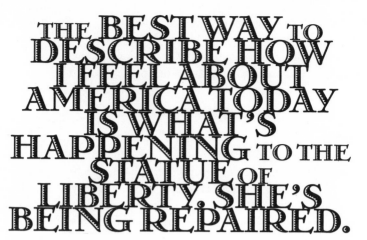

THE BEST WAY TO
DESCRIBE HOW
I FEEL ABOUT
AMERICA TODAY
IS WHAT'S
HAPPENING TO THE
STATUE OF
LIBERTY. SHE'S
BEING REPAIRED.

—WAYLON JENNINGS, 1984

FRIENDS & RIVALS

SIDEKICKS: FRIENDS IN LOW PLACES

I've got them trained to do what I tell them.

—JOHNNY CASH, on recording with the Highwaymen:
Willie Nelson, Waylon Jennings, and Kris Kristofferson, 1993

Willie Nelson is my buddy, but I may have to shoot him one of these days. —WAYLON JENNINGS, 1994

Willie's the old coyote, Waylon's the riverboat gambler, I'm the radical revolutionary, and Johnny's the father of our country.

—KRIS KRISTOFFERSON, 1994

I can outparty Waylon, but Kris, he makes it a religion. Waylon, in his old age, he'd run anybody a race for their money. But since he's quit drugs, he's very boring. He's reliable and all that shit. He shows up, he sings good. Who needs that? —WILLIE NELSON, 1995

It was almost like tying two cats' tails together and throwing them over a clothesline. We didn't know what might happen. It turned out to be a good thing. We were in each other's face 24 hours a day. We *had* to work it out. —WYNONNA JUDD, on working with her mother, Naomi, 1993

It was death and rebirth. I didn't feel I had any identity as Wynonna. I was in shock, and I didn't feel I had any right to carry on without her; Mom had worked so hard, and I was just "Naomi's kid." —WYNONNA JUDD, on going solo, 1993

I never been so scared in my life. Wouldn't you know, somebody yelled, "Where's George?" I shook for about five seconds and pretended not to hear. Then I got to where later on I'd joke about it. I'd say, "I don't know where he is, and he doesn't know either."

—TAMMY WYNETTE, on performing without George Jones, 1993

It was just kind of, you know, "Do your deal, and I'll do my deal. And we'll just see how far it goes."

—RONNIE DUNN, of Brooks & Dunn, on his and Kix's stylistic differences, 1996

When we came to Nashville, our hair was long, we didn't sound like everybody else, we didn't look like everybody else. [The other artists] would look at us like, "Hey, what's this about?" But Chet [Atkins] would talk to us, and they'd see Chet talking to us, they'd say, "Well, these are Chet's friends. We'll give 'em a chance. Let's not chase 'em out of town yet." You didn't want to upset Chet; he was top dog then, too.   —DON EVERLY, of the Everly Brothers, 1996

> # SHOTGUN RED IS AS REAL TO ME AS ANY OF THESE GUESTS SITTING ON THIS COUCH. AS FAR AS I'M CONCERNED, SHOTGUN RED SPEAKS FOR SHOTGUN RED.
>
> —RALPH EMERY, radio personality and host of *Nashville Now*, when asked who is the voice for Shotgun Red, 1991

In all these years, Minnie Pearl never hurt anybody's feelings, because she was a thoroughly nice person. She still is. She never faced any abrasive situations. She didn't do the traveling. She laid dormant in the garment bag, and when she came onstage, she was rested.

—SARAH OPHELIA CALLEY CANNON, aka Minnie Pearl (1912–1996), 1988

It's hard for me, at my age, to make new buddies. There's nothing like old friends, and that's old as in "o-l-e." It's hard for me to open up to people when I first meet 'em because I can't play that game.

—LORRIE MORGAN, 1996

MY HEROES HAVE ALWAYS BEEN COWBOYS

I don't think an entertainer is anybody without his heroes.
—GARTH BROOKS, 1995

My mama told me once, "I worry about you. All your heroes are either convicts, drug addicts, or outlaws!" And that's the truth. I'm talkin' Jesse James to Bob Dylan. Hank Williams to Jesus Christ. Willie Nelson, Johnny Cash.
—MARTY STUART, 1996

Nobody fills Merle Haggard's shoes, and anyone that tries is a fool.
—MARTY HAGGARD, Merle Haggard's son, 1996

I guess I've come to realize as time goes on, that the nut doesn't fall far from the tree, and that probably the greatest influence on me was my own dad, Mel Tillis.
—PAM TILLIS, 1996

Hank Williams is like a Cadillac. He'll always be the standard for comparison.
—JOHNNY CASH

Hank Williams had a way of reaching your guts and head at the same time. No matter who you were, a country person or a sophisticate, the language hit home.
—MITCH MILLER

You could hear a pin drop when Hank [Williams] was working. He seemed to hypnotize those people. You couldn't put your finger on the reason. Simplicity, I guess. He brought the people with him, put himself on their level.
—LITTLE JIMMY DICKENS

[Hank Williams] destroyed the women in the audience. They just had to have his autograph and get close enough to touch him. It wasn't sex, per se, like with some artists. He appealed to their maternal instincts. —MINNIE PEARL (1912–1996)

[Minnie Pearl's] work is timeless. Her "Howdy!" is timeless. The laughter she caused people to have, and the goodwill she spread . . . that's timeless. That's gonna live way on, beyond all of us. We're lucky we have footage of her, miles of footage. We can visit her anytime we want to. —MARTY STUART, 1996

[Minnie Pearl] had insight into people's souls and feelings, and a wonderful awareness of the silliness—and poignancy—involved in taking ourselves too seriously. —DWIGHT YOAKAM, 1996

Whether they know it or not, the new guys, they may have never heard of Jimmie Rodgers, but they definitely are influenced by [him]. They have to be if they're singing country music.
—WAYLON JENNINGS, 1996

I helped [Patsy Cline] with her stage presence. Patsy wanted to play the guitar. I told her, "Throw that fucking thing away and get that mike and start walking with it. As long as you're moving, they're gonna watch you. If you stand still, no one's gonna pay you any mind." —FARON YOUNG (1932–1996), 1993

[Patsy Cline] was tougher than the back end of a shootin' gallery. And if she got mad, she could say words that would wilt grass.
—JIMMY DEAN, 1996

Patsy [Cline] is still around because she is what we all want to be— a real star. And people can't get enough of a real star.
—DOTTIE WEST (1932–1991)

Dottie West was one of those people who believed what she sang. If she sang "Country Sunshine," you felt country sunshine. If she sang about pain, you could see it in her face, you could feel it in her voice.　　　　　　　　　　　　　　　　　　　　　—KENNY ROGERS, 1996

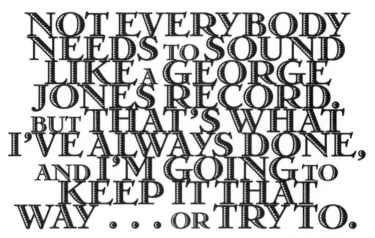

NOT EVERYBODY NEEDS TO SOUND LIKE A GEORGE JONES RECORD. BUT THAT'S WHAT I'VE ALWAYS DONE, AND I'M GOING TO KEEP IT THAT WAY . . . OR TRY TO.

—ALAN JACKSON, 1996

All the new, hot country artists have been so nice to me. Vince Gill, Marty Stuart, Alan Jackson, they've kept me goin' in country music. Makes me feel 20 years younger.　　　—GEORGE JONES, 1995

[Elvis] told me that I was his favorite singer. Later on, when he got big, he changed. Frank Sinatra and Perry Como were his favorite singers. But I think Colonel Tom Parker had something to do with that, because I don't believe they would allow Presley to really become involved with country music, because it would bring him down. And he loved country music. He knew all the songs. He knew everybody's songs.

　　　—MARTY ROBBINS (1925–1982), on Elvis Presley and his oppressive manager, Tom Parker

If someone mentioned Merle Haggard, Johnny Cash, and Bob Wills, I'd be flattered. Those are the people I grew up listening to, and that's the music that influenced me. If you can hear Lefty, Faron, and Waylon [in my songs], it means I'm stayin' on the right track.　　　　　　　　—DALE WATSON, singer-songwriter, 1995

[Johnny Cash] [He] comes in a room, you don't have to see or hear him to know he's there. Hell, people who don't know country from cornflakes know Johnny Cash

—KRIS KRISTOFFERSON, 1993

Lester [Flatt] and Johnny [Cash] weren't the kind of guys who set you down and talked to you. You just watched the way they conducted life.

—MARTY STUART, 1994

[Johnny] Cash taught me that not everyone born in places like Kingsland, Arkansas, where people work with their hands and talk like L. B. J., [is] a beady-eyed racist standing behind a luncheonette counter with an ax handle. Cash taught me it was possible for a white man inflamed with the Pentecostal spirit—some damn Jesus shouter!—to be not only smarter than a wiseacre like me but cooler, too.

—MARK JACOBSON, journalist, 1994

Country music is soul. And soul is Jessi Colter. She's got such a beautiful outlook on life that I think she was born half high.

—WAYLON JENNINGS, on his wife, Jessi Colter, 1975

I wanted to be like Gene Autry. I wanted to ride off into the sunset. And then later on I found out that Gene owns the sunset, and I couldn't ride off into it unless I asked him. So I settled on being a country and western singer.

—MARTY ROBBINS (1925–1982)

> HE WAS A SUCCESSFUL SINGER AND ALL OF THAT, BUT AS FAR AS THE SONG-WRITING AND THE KIND OF VISION THAT HE HAD, HE WAS A PRETTY SOULFUL CAT.
>
> —DAVE ALVIN, singer-songwriter, on Marty Robbins, 1995

I think he was a down-home person, enjoyed people. He enjoyed the ability he had. Not that he showed it off, but he didn't mind sharin' it with people.

—RICHARD PETTY, race-car driver, on Marty Robbins, 1995

[Buddy Holly was] a very rare talent who made over 40 records, a lot of which he wrote, all in two years. I mean, that star was shining brightly. Who knows what would've happened after that. I mean, he died at the age of 22. Twenty-two! . . . and there's all this [music left behind].

—DAVE EDMUNDS, 1996

I've never admitted this before, but one of my great Buddy Holly memories was standing in front of a mirror with a tennis racquet, playin' along with "Oh Boy," and "Peggy Sue."

—JIMMY IBBOTSON, of the Nitty Gritty Dirt Band, 1996

I like Buddy [Holly's] music 'cause it had a smile on it.

—MARTY STUART, 1996

[Marty Stuart's] a good all-around musician. His instrument is the mandolin, but he's a great guitar player. He's better than he thinks he is, and he thinks he's pretty good. —JOHNNY CASH, 1994

[When] this man opens his mouth, it's a party!

—PAM TILLIS, on Delbert McClinton, 1996

[Gus Hardin's] voice was full of testimony.

—DELBERT McCLINTON, 1996

[Leon Russell] said I sounded like a combination of Tammy Wynette, Otis Redding, and a truck driver.

—GUS HARDIN (1945–1996)

[Marty Brown] is the sweetest surprise to ride the train in a long, long time, and so authentically country he probably still has a tick in his navel. —*Entertainment Weekly*, 1993

He's the kind of guy you'd want to take home to meet your father, *if* you could trust your mother. —BUCK OWENS, on Clint Black, 1993

I love Kenny [Rogers's] voice 'cause I can feel it. It's very emotional. It comes from a very deep place. Plus it had a jarring kind of vibrating sound that touches women, I know. I don't know how men feel, but it *stirs* me. I think it's sexy!

—DOLLY PARTON, 1996

If Randy Travis had come to Nashville last month, he probably wouldn't have gotten a record deal. He's too good and too original. And he doesn't wear a hat or pimple cream.

—GEORGE JONES, 1996

I think Alison [Krauss] is terrified of me because I blow in the door like a hurricane and suck up all the oxygen in the room. I wear my heart on my sleeve and say whatever comes to my mind. But Alison is this quiet, sweet person who thinks about what she says before she says it. —WYNONNA JUDD, 1996

If they sing country music in heaven, there's a good chance that the angels sound like the Everly Brothers.

—*The Life and Times of the Everly Brothers*, 1996

[The Everly Brothers] had such a tight, clean, pure harmony. It had an innocence about it. It was so fresh. It was like slicing a spring tomato.

—FELICE BRYANT, surviving half of the songwriting team Felice
and Boudleaux Bryant, who created many Everly Brothers hits, 1996

HOW COULD YOU NOT LIKE HER? THE WOMAN IS HUMAN SUNSHINE.

—BURT REYNOLDS, on Dolly Parton, 1989

Dolly was the real thing: She'd lived that life. She crawled out of her cradle singing that music. —LINDA RONSTADT, 1993

There's really only three female singers in the world: Streisand, Ronstadt, and Connie Smith. The rest of us are only pretending.
—DOLLY PARTON, 1993

Connie Smith can wrap her tonsils around a song as good as anybody. —BILL ANDERSON, 1996

She came onto the scene a little bit different, because she came in kinda from the underground side. But she's as country as a can o' kraut. —JEANNE PRUETT, on Emmylou Harris, 1993

She sure seriously dilutes the ugly up here!
—STEVE EARLE, onstage with Emmylou Harris, 1996

There's something about the way [Steve Earle] writes that is incredible. His songs are . . . almost evil. —WADE HAYES, 1996

[Tennessee Ernie Ford] was a man, a full-blown man, full-blown talent, and he used those things to make a wonderful life. I don't know what he did for music, quote-unquote. . . . And I don't think he cared too much about that, really. I think he was about using his talent, living his life, and the devil take the hind parts.
—DELLA REESE, 1996

Ernest Tubb had a sincerity in the way he read the lyric. That was his identity. —OWEN BRADLEY, record producer, 1996

[Ernest Tubb] loved his fellow performers. And anything that [he] could do to help anybody, especially the young performers coming into the business. Any advice he could give them . . . he was always there. —JEAN SHEPARD, 1996

I've learned more in 30 minutes of singin' with Loretta Lynn than I've learned from a handful of vocal coaches. —PAM TILLIS, 1996

No matter what trends come to dominate country music, there will probably always be a market for Loretta Lynn. Her voice is quirky, graceful, and enormously expressive, an instrument worthy of national treasure status.

—ALANNA NASH, music journalist, 1996

[Travis Tritt is] a great singer. He don't try to sing beautiful, he's like me. He just opens up and lets it fly. If it comes out wrong, it just does. —LORETTA LYNN, 1995

I saw [Reba McEntire's] show, and I knew right then and there what I was going to be doing for the rest of my life. So when I was backstage getting an autograph, I was totally speechless, but as I was walking away I just turned around and said, "I love you, Reba McEntire!" And she said, "I love you, too, honey." I have the picture from that evening. —FAITH HILL, 1996

Alongside Hank Williams, he's truly one of the greatest poets we've ever had. —MARTY STUART, on Merle Haggard, 1996

[Merle Haggard] is just as cool as ice, you know. He walks out there [onstage] and stands in his place, and he doesn't even know what he's going to be playing. He just starts banging on that ol' Telecaster and singing whatever comes to mind. He's a classic.

—ALAN JACKSON, 1994

[Lefty Frizzell's] voice was like a raindrop. Almost like Judy Garland or something. [He was] somebody very, very special with a gift in [his] throat. —MERLE HAGGARD, 1996

I met with [Billy Ray Cyrus] back in the summer, and we did some concerts. That was when "Achy Breaky" was right at its peak, and he was just as cute as he could be, so impressed to be working with Dolly Parton, who'd been in music for a hundred years. So he was asking my advice, pretty much like my brother or a nephew. . . . I found him a very kind and generous soul, so it worked out real well.

—DOLLY PARTON, 1993

[Garth] Brooks has a knack for telling people the things they need to hear. He's given to bold, sweeping statements. . . . But that's part of what got him where he is. It's part of what fuels his music, where he takes the commonplace—country music, with all its emphasis on small towns, basic values, and traditions—and turns it into something grand and mythical. A rodeo rider isn't just a cowboy, he's a fever-driven lunatic with a death wish.

—BRIAN MANSFIELD, journalist, 1996

> # WE WERE COMING AT THE SONG-WRITING THING FROM A COUPLE DIFFERENT PERSPECTIVES. HE'S ONE OF THE NEW, YOUNG GUYS, AND I BEEN HERE SINCE DIRT.
> —BILL ANDERSON, on writing and recording with Vince Gill, 1995

I think anytime you work with [another artist] more than in a sort of a superficial way, you pick things up, you absorb it like a sponge. That relationship is so intuitive in so many ways. There's reflections of it from then on.   —MARY CHAPIN CARPENTER, 1996

I had just had my twenty-fourth birthday when we made that album and I didn't have a clue. Every day I was getting to be in the studio and sing and play with my heroes and I didn't care if anybody bought it.

—JEFF HANNA, of the Nitty Gritty Dirt Band, on
recording "Will the Circle Be Unbroken" with
country music legends, including Roy Acuff
and the Carter Family, 1995

[Roy Acuff] to me was like one of them East Tennessee mountain streams. It's just as pure water as you'll ever find.

—MARTY STUART, 1996

Roy [Acuff] was one of the greatest communicators of a line. He'd get up and sing one of them songs, "Wreck on the Highway," or "Great Speckled Bird," and the tears would come out his eyes.

—CHET ATKINS, 1996

Anyone who likes Bob Wills's music is bound to have some good in them.

—ANN COKER, journalist, 1996

I didn't realize how white I was till I got beside him and tried to sing.

—RICKY SKAGGS, on Sam Moore of the '60s R&B group Sam and Dave, 1996

In a sea of tight britches and cowboy hats, Ricky [Skaggs] had been kind of overlooked.

—MARTY STUART, 1996

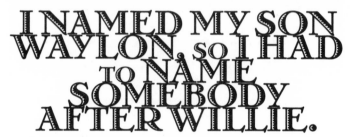

I NAMED MY SON WAYLON, SO I HAD TO NAME SOMEBODY AFTER WILLIE.

—MARK CHESNUTT, on naming his miniature Doberman pinscher after Willie Nelson, 1996

Dwight's different. Dwight stands out. He's a good writer, a good picker. He's smart. He's gonna be around for a long time.

—WILLIE NELSON, on Dwight Yoakam, 1996

[Dwight] Yoakam dares to be different. I see a lot of myself in him, and I appreciate him—I think he's probably better than a dirt sandwich.

—JOHNNY CASH, 1994

Dwight [Yoakam] is one of my favorite artists of the past 15 years. He's fiercely original, unafraid to stretch the boundaries, and he has a high cool factor wrapped in integrity.

—MARTY STUART, 1996

The best-armed New Age hard-core honky tonk tee-totaling metaphysabilly I know.

—PATRICK CARR, journalist, on Dwight Yoakam, 1995

I come from that time when music just exploded on AM radio. You would hear Buck Owens come right behind the Beatles or the Stones, and lead into Them with Van Morrison, and then go into maybe the Statler Brothers, doin' "Flowers on the Wall." Henson Cargill doin' "Skip a Rope." *Everything* was going on.

—DWIGHT YOAKAM, 1995

I've got four older brothers. They all loved James Taylor. Seventy-one, *Sweet Baby James, Mud Slide Slim* started coming into the house. That's when it started for me, as a kid.

—GARTH BROOKS, 1996

Garth Brooks, average guy, pleasant singer and hokey holy terror as a performer, is the surprising new face of pop. . . . Here is this unlikely new country superstar, with his acetylene eyes and chipmunk cheeks, stalking the concert stage, acting up, acting crazy, climbing the rigging and blitzing the crowd with bravura. He's part Jolson and part Jagger, pulling stunts that smack more of the Fillmore than the Opry, and the audience hollers for him, feasts on him, lets itself go nuts with him. Nicely nuts. Mannerly nuts. Country nuts. —JAY COCKS, *Time* (CD Rom), 1994

I was four or five years old [when I first heard the banjo]. My brother and I were on my grandparents' bed watching TV when *The Beverly Hillbillies* came on. The theme music started, and I had no idea it was the banjo. It was Earl Scruggs in his prime. I only remember hearing something beautiful. It called out to me.

—BELA FLECK, 1994

Nashville had its sound, but there was something about the West Coast sound that always attracted me, and Buck Owens was an innovator of that style. It rocked, it was edgy, it had Nudie suits, Fender Telecasters, cool cowboy boots, and it twanged real hard.

—MARTY STUART, 1996

[Our white congregation sang] from the same hymnals [as the blacks], but we weren't singing the same songs. Black phrasing had all these bends and sweeps and curls, using your voice more like a musical instrument. When I tried it, I discovered something else very strange . . . I could sing that way. In fact, that was the way I was supposed to sing.   —TRAVIS TRITT, 1994

> I'VE WORKED WITH JUST ABOUT EVERYBODY THERE IS. I'VE MET MY HEROES AND SUNG WITH MOST OF THEM. WHO'S LEFT?
>
> —ALAN JACKSON, 1995

H[ank Williams] kept sayin', "My throat's sore. I can't record right now." And [the record people] kept callin', wanting him to record somethin', and finally they said, "What the hell is it gonna take to cure you of your sore throat?" And he said, "About twenty-five thousand ought to do it."

—CHET ATKINS, on Hank Williams, 1988

There's a lot of people that love to tell you Hank Williams stories, and they ain't never seen him. He was here in '49 and he was gone in '53. That's it. Ernest Tubb summed it up perfectly—"If he'da had a drink and gone to school with everybody who says he did, he'd have been the most educated alcoholic in the world."

—HANK WILLIAMS, JR., 1988

The character of Minnie Pearl is a blend of brash and beautiful. She is the man-hungry old maid with a coy demeanor and a glint in her eye. She is the homely wallflower with just enough pluck and grit to keep her chin up. She's small-town gossip without malice, bubbling with news of Uncle Nabob, Aunt Ambrosy, Brother, Lizzie Tinkum, and the other characters who inhabit her fictional Grinders Switch neighborhood.

—MARY A. BUFWACK AND ROBERT K. OERMANN,
Finding Her Voice: The Saga of Women in Country Music

I remember one time Elvis [Presley] started jumpin' around and split his pants right in the seat, don't you know, and he asked somebody to run to the hotel and get him another pair. I'll never forget them—they were pink with black piping on the sides. He changed his pants and left the old ones behind, layin' around somewhere. Some girl who worked there found them and said, "What am I suppose to do with these pants?" I said, "Keep 'em. They'll be worth a lot of money one day." And she thought that was funny, but six months later I heard she was trying to get on *I've Got a Secret*.

—CHET ATKINS, 1988

I'd get my car, and he'd make a deal to get me a date with his girlfriend's girlfriend. Most of the time we'd go out on the levee, by the Mississippi River, and he'd sit down, start playin' his guitar. I'd sit over there and be tryin' to make out. "That Harold Jenkins, he's kinda crazy. He's got a problem, him playin' that guitar. He oughta be flirtin' with his girl." Well, needless to say, I shoulda been playin' the guitar myself.

—HUGH CARDEN, longtime friend of Conway Twitty (born Harold Jenkins), 1996

I remember Loretta [Lynn] was standing there facing Owen [Bradley], and I was standing right behind her. He said, "Do you still want to meet Conway Twitty?" And she said, "Yeah!" And he said, "Well, he's right behind you." She turned around, and she jumped straight up! She's a character anyway, you know. She was just slappin' her leg, and sayin', "I can't believe it! I met Conway Twitty." We were friends really, right off the bat.

—CONWAY TWITTY (1933–1993)

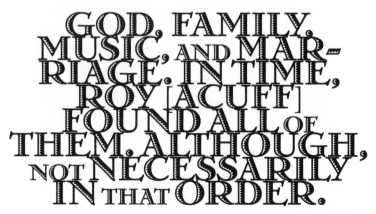

GOD, FAMILY, MUSIC, AND MARRIAGE. IN TIME, ROY [ACUFF] FOUND ALL OF THEM, ALTHOUGH, NOT NECESSARILY IN THAT ORDER.

—HOYT AXTON, 1996

Legend has it that Marines in the Pacific [during World War II] heard Japanese soldiers taunting them by shouting, "To hell with Roosevelt! To hell with Babe Ruth! To hell with Roy Acuff!"

—BRUCE HONICK, journalist, 1996

Back in [the 1930s] there was a saying, that people would go in a store and buy a loaf of bread, eggs, milk and the latest Jimmie Rodgers record. 'Cause it kept them going.

—JIMMIE DALE COURT, Jimmie Rodgers's grandson, 1996

I walked over and opened up my pocket knife and scratched a big cross on his mandolin. And he said, "Why'd you do that?" And I said, "Because Jesus loves you. Don't forget it."

—JOHNNY CASH, on Marty Stuart, 1993

Merle Haggard was on a bill with us at a fair. I said to someone, "Man, before he goes onstage, please take my guitar and get him to sign it." The word came back, "You can have his autograph, but you have to come get it yourself. . . ." So I get my guitar and suck up all my courage. I felt like Dorothy walking up to see the Wizard of Oz. I was scared to death. And it turned out to be . . . the greatest 15 minutes of my life. —KIX BROOKS, of Brooks & Dunn, 1996

I called [Bill Monroe] and asked if he'd [record with us], and he said, "What tune are you gonna play?" I said, " 'Molly and Tenbrooks.' " He said, "I'll be right over." I think he mainly wanted to be there to make sure I didn't screw up his song. —TOM T. HALL, 1993

When you talk about [Bill] Monroe, you're talkin' about a different kind of human being. You've never seen anybody like him in your life, and you never will. He's a hard man, and strength and power is his leader. If you're not strong, you're not worthy. And you've got to prove to him that you're strong.

—SONNY OSBORNE, of the Osborne Brothers, 1996

A bunch of us musicians went into Juarez, Mexico, after a Faron Young date in El Paso. Patsy [Cline] tagged along. The guys bought a little grass, then worried how they were going to get it back across the border. Nothing scared Patsy. She said, "What the hell y'all worried about when you got the Cline here? Give me that stuff. I'll take care of it." And she grabbed it and stuffed it down her bra. She was cool as a cucumber as we crossed the border. She never even held her breath. —ROGER MILLER (1936–1992)

When I was on the road as a kid with Faron [Young], Mel Tillis, and George Jones, they'd tell me jokes—none of which I understood. Then they'd say, "Hey, Brenda, go tell so-and-so that." And I'd go up to someone and do it. They'd say, "Lord, all that coming out of a kid's mouth!" The guys were on the floor laughing.

—BRENDA LEE, 1993

[In 1987] one of those supermarket newspapers had a full-page story about the face of Jesus suddenly appearing on the outside wall of a grocery store in South America after a dramatic rainstorm. Hundreds of people came to pray to the image of Jesus, and some of the sick went home cured. A few days later, following another thunderstorm, a new figure appeared on the wall beside Jesus. It was Julio Iglesias. What had happened, the rain had washed off the coat of whitewash that had covered a poster for "To All the Girls I've Loved Before." The supermarket [newspaper] headline read: "That's not Jesus—it's just old Willie." —WILLIE NELSON, 1988

Reportedly, Willie Nelson needed money and tried to sell ["Hello Walls"]. Faron Young persuaded Willie to keep his copyright and loaned him $500 instead. According to Faron, [after receiving] the first $3,000 royalty check for "Hello Walls," Willie tracked Faron down and kissed him . . . flush on the mouth.

—*Opry Backstage*, 1996

Johnny [Darrell] was real drunk. He snatched up Willie [Nelson's] Martin guitar—the famous one he picked so much he wore a hole in it, the one with all the names signed on it. . . . Very nicely, Willie said, "Johnny, if you don't mind, would you please use another guitar?" Johnny ignored him and went right on tuning and flogging the guitar and stumbling around. Willie said, "Johnny, please. There's plenty of guitars in this room, but that one is very special to me. I'm afraid you're gonna break it." Darrell whirled on him and said, "What's the matter? You become too goddamn big a star to let me use your guitar?" Willie was off that couch like a shot and across the room and grabbed Darrell and pinned him against the wall in the corner and said very quietly but forcefully, "Put that guitar down and do it now." Johnny immediately put down the guitar. Willie went back and sat on the couch, gave one of his serene smiles, and said, "Now, then, I'd sure like to hear your songs, Johnny." —CHARLIE WILLIAMS, songwriter and producer, 1988

Once when I was trying to stay sober, the owner of a Baltimore nightclub insisted on having a drink with me. "I'm paying the bills around here, and I've given George Jones a week's worth of work," he said. "Does he think he's too good to drink with me?" So after my last show I told him, "Okay, my friend. Break out the bottle." We killed a fifth of whiskey and got into another. Then I got out of my mind. I threw an ashtray at a mirror behind the bar, and glass flew in all directions. I broke glasses, smashed mirrors, bent metal chairs, broke the legs off tables, tore down curtains, and shattered whiskey bottles. The club owner jumped on me and I beat the hell out of him. I'm glad I had already been paid for my week's work.

—GEORGE JONES, 1996

Ernest refused to press charges against a drifter who broke into his bus. Instead, he asked him why he did it. He then lent him the $200 the man said he was trying to raise for bus fare to rejoin his family. Months later, in Florida, with his family in tow, the man knocked on the door of the Troubadours' bus and repaid the $200. Ernest was the only one on the bus who didn't seem surprised. Instead, he handed the money back to the man, saying, "Your pretty little girls look like they'd enjoy new dresses."

—RONNIE PUGH, *The Life and Times of Ernest Tubb*, 1996

[Webb Pierce's] lifestyle was a valentine to honky-tonk expression. He built the first guitar-shaped swimming pool, and drove a

Cadillac that was lined with silver dollars and sported six-shooters for door handles.

—RICKY SKAGGS, 1996

As popular as he was on records, in person Bob Wills and his Texas Playboys were nothing less than a sensation. He'd holler to his band in a strange, high-pitched voice, the way he'd heard the old black blues singers do back in the cotton camps of east Texas. He had worked beside them in the fields and then made music with them in the evenings. Bob Wills had been there; he was the real thing.

—*The Life and Times of Bob Wills*

[Dottie West] had just met some young songwriters, all men, and they'd all started hanging around together, often at her house. There was young Kris Kristofferson, Willie Nelson, Roger Miller. They were all undiscovered, all struggling, all hungry. Dottie said her cooking made her a better songwriter.

—*The Life and Times of Dottie West*

To me, your Garth Brooks, Reba McEntire, some of your people like that, have used country music as a stepping-stone. They've come in with a label when they first start off recording, they have 'em a couple big hits that are pure country songs . . . and then, about the next album they cut, they've changed overnight. They got dollar signs all through their brains. They jump up, and all of a sudden they're so pop it's pitiful.

—GEORGE JONES, 1995

> ## [DWIGHT YOAKAM] USED TO BE A HILLBILLY SINGER, BUT LOOK AT HIM NOW! [NASHVILLE] RUINED HIM.
> —WAYNE HANCOCK, 1996

I want you to know Travis Tritt is the only person who's ever brought his hair dryer to the Broken Spoke.

—MARTY STUART, at Austin's Broken Spoke honky-tonk, 1995

I think it degrades country music. It comes out and it says that everybody in country music, instead of producing songs that really get to the heart of the matter and really talk to the public, it says . . . what we're going to have to do in country music is get into an ass wigglin' contest with one another.

—TRAVIS TRITT, on Billy Ray Cyrus's hit, "Achy Breaky Heart," 1994

I call [Travis Tritt] Mr. Twitt. He's just jealous 'cause his records don't sell what Billy Ray sells, and when he gets up in the mornin' and looks in the mirror, he don't see what Billy Ray sees.

—A Billy Ray Cyrus staff member, 1993

I know what the deal is. And I know that *they* know, and they know that *I* know. *You* know. Shoot, man. I'm just proud of the music and what it's done, and I really don't need somebody to hand me a trophy and tell me that this music did something big. I could see that for myself.

—BILLY RAY CYRUS, on the lack of acknowledgment from the Country Music Association, 1995

Billy Ray [Cyrus], he's not a good singer, but he don't need to be if you look that good.   —WAYLON JENNINGS, 1993

Watching [Billy Ray Cyrus] at a taping at TNN's studios trying to hold up his end of a conversation with *Music City Tonight* hosts Lorianne Crook and Charlie Chase is almost as painful as listening to anything from his latest album, *Storm in the Heartland.*

—BILLY ALTMAN, *GQ,* 1996

About the mid-70s, I started getting very pissed off at country music and stopped listening to 'em totally. . . . What they play are these pretty boys with hair longer than my momma's! I know it's not nice to slam Nashville, but forgive me. I'm gonna slam 'em anyway, 'cause they need to be slammed. They need to be woke up.

—WAYNE HANCOCK, 1996

Tanya? She still thinks asphalt is bowel trouble.

—GLEN CAMPBELL, on Tanya Tucker, 1988

SHE HEAPED a LOT OF CRAP IN THAT BOOK OF HERS.

—JEAN SHEPARD, on Loretta Lynn's autobiography,
in which she bad-mouthed the Opry girl singers, 1993

If a woman had stolen my husband, I wouldn't be confessing it like that. Yes, neither Charlie [Battles] or Narvel [Blackstock] were separated from their wives when I met them, but they were unhappy in those marriages. I didn't "steal" 'em! I don't feel guilty about that one bit!

—REBA McENTIRE, on being called a home wrecker, 1996

The only song Tug [McGraw] knows is the national anthem, and he still thinks Elvis is alive.

—TIM McGRAW, on his father, 1994

Bill [McCall] was the craftiest operator I'd seen in my life. A Californian in the truest sense of the word—suave, delightful, and he could charm the pants right off your behind while he stabbed you in the back. Anyone who signed with him—writers, singers—he nailed to the wall. He was a shyster from the word go.

—JIMMY DEAN, on the Four Star Records executive who signed Patsy Cline, 1993

[Bill] McCall paid [for dinner] that night, but it ended up being on me. I paid for every goddamned thing from then on. I didn't know how much till it was too late.

—PATSY CLINE (1932–1963)

Joey Bishop and his big baloney about how he loved country music . . . that's the biggest joke in the world. I played his show and I tried to get him to take my part off [his program] 'cause I stood there singing madder than a son of a bitch.

—WAYLON JENNINGS, on Joey Bishop's mocking portrayal of country music, 1971

Now they're beautiful children, and they're very talented, but they wouldn't know a country song if it hit 'em in the hind end with a broom handle!

—JEAN SHEPARD, on Donny and Marie Osmond, 1993

You either did it the way Bill wanted it, or you look for something else to do.

—ROBERT "CHUBBY" WISE (1915–1996), fiddle player for Bill Monroe's Bluegrass Boys

~157

... pea-brained intellectuals [and] fledgling bigots ... academics who are as dumb as a box of rats when it comes to living. They can stay away and kisseth all the hind parts I can't reach.

—CHARLIE DANIELS, referring to the college students who protested Daniels's addressing the North Carolina, Wilmington, class of '96, 1996

I'VE BEEN IN MORE THAN ONE "STAR" SESSION WHEN YOU NEEDED A CHAINSAW, NEVER MIND A KNIFE, TO CUT THROUGH THE ATMOSPHERE.

—PATRICK CARR, journalist, on country stars with attitudes, 1993

WOMEN IN COUNTRY

DON'T COME HOME
A'DRINKIN' WITH LOVIN'
ON YOUR MIND

Before, a lot of women identified with "Don't Come Home A'Drinkin' with Lovin' on Your Mind." Now, it's "Don't even think about comin' home, 'cause I ain't gonna be here."
—REBA McENTIRE

Country music was always about real life, and hopefully we'll come back to that. It dealt with everything from death to murder, cheating, drinking—life as we see it. Leave it to Loretta Lynn to write "Don't Come Home A'Drinkin' with Lovin' on Your Mind." If that's not the real world for a lot of women, I don't know what is.
—RADNEY FOSTER, 1995

I put my career before my children when I first came to Nashville. If I had put my children first, we'd have starved to death. I did what I had to do, what I was forced to do. I did a lot of things women wouldn't attempt to do.
—TAMMY WYNETTE, 1988

I don't know if you're aware of it, but there's this big national trend for women who have figured out that it's not as satisfying out there as they maybe dreamed it would be. And that the most satisfying roll of all, the most rewarding in every which way, is to be there for [your children] when they really need you.
—NAOMI JUDD, 1996

Someday . . . I'll be able to draw in a coliseum the way that a man does, *if* I stay true to what I believe people need and want to hear. Because women buy most of the records. And just because some folks want to see women as victims forever and forever does *not* mean that that's what they will always be.

—LACY J. DALTON, 1988

Not only are the women [artists] in competition with the men, but they're in competition with all sorts of forms of entertainment. Basketball games, movies, rock 'n' roll. So it takes a lot of hard work and energy to make sure that you put on the best show possible, that when your show comes to town and it's either you or a basketball game, they say, "Man, let's go see Reba."

—REBA McENTIRE, 1995

Reba [McEntire] made it easier for somebody like me to get respect as a businesswoman and not only as a pretty little miss. Reba is the ultimate businesswoman.

—TRISHA YEARWOOD, 1995

I've got to be a businesswoman, a mother, a star, a singer, a down-to-earth person who brings the crew chili. I've got to be everything, and sometimes that's damned hard.

—TANYA TUCKER, 1994

I had to be tough—in the good sense—because I've had a lot of hard knocks. . . . But what man out there isn't tough? You've got to stand up for what you believe. If I hadn't been tough in this town, I wouldn't be where I am.

—LORRIE MORGAN, 1996

There's a strong side of me that I'm only still discovering, the kind of business and military instincts that was called "masculine," for lack of a better word. When the feminist movement began in the '60s, I was shocked to find it was such a big issue.

—BARBARA MANDRELL

I'm not fierce about feminism, but I am firm about being a strong person. So many people think feminism means giving up things that make men and women different and interesting to each other. I don't think that's so.

—KATHY MATTEA

IT'S A LONELY BUSINESS, BEIN' BALLSY.

—TANYA TUCKER, 1993

When I first came to Nashville, the industry was not open to a woman . . . having too much to say about the production. But I feel strongly about my music, and I don't believe being firm about my convictions and standing up for them is in conflict with my femininity. —GAIL DAVIES, 1993

The same men [in the country music industry] who treated wives and girlfriends with respect and consideration treated girl singers like a piece of merchandise. We had to be professional, prompt and always ladylike. But we also had to be tough enough to stand up for ourselves. Every career woman knows the fine line you walk to succeed. —TAMMY WYNETTE, 1993

I used to work clubs, and often the attitude was that if they booked you, they owned you as a woman. They bought you to play the club. They bought you, period. It didn't take much to set them straight, but it hurt just the same. —CONNIE SMITH, 1993

Women tend to embrace the emotional communication aspect of our music better than men. —ED BENSON, executive director of the Country Music Association, 1996

Women haven't sold in the past because men told them what to sing. —JIMMY BOWEN, former president of Liberty Records, 1993

Most male artists are still pretty traditional—the women are pushing the envelope. —TONY BROWN, president of MCA Records in Nashville, 1995

You know, I think it's a deal of when you've been down, or the underdog, so to speak, you have less to lose. So women are taking risks musically. We have less to lose. —PAM TILLIS, 1996

The female [artists] are less restrictive, creatively, and I think they've had a little more freedom to experiment and to do some things. Even historically, I don't think this is anything new.

—WADE JESSEN, manager of the *Billboard* country charts, 1996

Every female [in today's country] has a real identity while 80 percent of the male artists are identical. To get heard on country radio, females have taken the angle of "I should sound different." Whereas the males, in order to get heard, say, "I should sound like everybody else so they'll play me."

—TONY BROWN, president of MCA Records in Nashville, 1996

It's a different business for a woman than it is for a man. A man can "come out of the box" and sell a million. On the other hand, the changing of the guard with the men is much quicker than it is for women. We're in the trenches slugging it out year after year. The guys tend to be more flashy. —HOLLY DUNN, 1993

> THERE'S A LOT OF GOOD-LOOKING
> WOMEN IN COUNTRY MUSIC RIGHT
> NOW, AND I LIKE THAT. I LIKE THE
> WAY THE WOMEN HAVE COME
> INTO THEIR OWN.
> —JOHNNY CASH, 1994

I do . . . interviews now, and they talk about how I was quite . . . what's the word for the new feminist movement? Liberated? Well, I didn't realize it at the time, but that's just it. My folks had raised me to think for myself. —WANDA JACKSON, 1993

I don't think you can say women have a hard time and they get less breaks than a man. You just gotta belly up to the bar and work harder. That's all you can do.

—REBA McENTIRE, 1995

There are times I feel like Charles Atlas, with the world on my shoulders. Men think they're stronger, but they're not. And true men will admit to that.

—TANYA TUCKER, 1994

Women are having more of a say and more of a place in life in general. We're stepping up and taking advantage of opportunities more and being our own best cheerleaders.

—HOLLY DUNN, 1996

I'm the girl singer, and that's a great job.

—REBA McENTIRE, 1995

I think it's just the '90s. Women are just getting ahead in every profession [in] this day and age. Music just happens to be one of those.

—SHANIA TWAIN, 1996

One of the virtues of these modern liberated times is that women can, in country music anyway, be sensitive, smart, aggressive and wholesome, all at the same time. You're never sure if you want to buy her a glass of milk or a double bourbon.

—MARY CHAPIN CARPENTER, 1993

I think a lot of women [in country music] have felt trapped for a long time, felt the need to conform to the sequined gowns and stuff. I'm aware of how alternative my looks are in comparison with other women. I get flak for it. . . . But what is paradoxical about it to me is that country's always been the vehicle for honesty. I've been like this my whole life.

—K. D. LANG

It's nice that people are noticing our material rather than asking us, "How does it feel to be a sex symbol?"

—LARI WHITE, 1996

I can't be pretty and sing. You know, I'm not one of those girls who can stand up there and not sweat and look beautiful. . . . I mean, I'm not very feminine.   —BRENDA LEE

Women in the country music of my daddy's era were so glamorous. They had the curls and the big hair and would waft along in a cloud of perfume. They were beautiful and when they sang, they were unforgettable.   —PAM TILLIS, 1996

Forget big hair and heartbreak. Country women have thoroughly transformed themselves in the 27 years since Tammy Wynette sang "Stand by Your Man" and meant it.

—SUZANNA ANDREWS, journalist, 1995

I didn't sing that song to say, "You women stay home and stay pregnant and don't do anything to help yourselves. Be there waiting when he comes home, because a woman needs a man at any costs." No, that's not what I was saying at all. . . . All I wanted to say in that song was "Be understanding. Be supportive."

—TAMMY WYNETTE, on criticism of her song, "Stand by Your Man"

There's a tough side of me that comes across in my songs—a side women seem to pick up on. Don't let this frilly look fool you.

—SHANIA TWAIN, 1995

There are some days when I feel like I could conquer the world, but—and I know the women's libbers are gonna hate me for this— there are other times when the woman in me comes out, when I feel weak and alone, and I feel like I need somebody to lean on.

—LORRIE MORGAN, 1993

The women's lib thing doesn't turn me on. I can't stand for a woman to stand up and say, "I can do anything a man can do." Maybe mentally she can. But I think it's still kind of a man's world, and to be frank, I kind of like it that way.

—JEAN SHEPARD, 1993

ANY WOMAN WHO SEEKS TO BE EQUAL TO A MAN HAS NO AMBITION.

—T. BUBBA BECHTOL, comic, 1995

Country music is a salve for the beleaguered housewife who grits her teeth as destiny dumps its slops on her head.

—Newsweek, 1971

[I am] a spokesperson for every woman who had gotten married too early, gotten pregnant too often, and felt trapped by the tedium and drudgery of her life. —LORETTA LYNN, 1996

[Women's] songs need to have the right tone, they can't be man-bashing. Guys like the songs I sing as much as women do, even if they are sung from a female perspective. . . . You don't want to alienate the male fan. —TERRI CLARK, 1996

I'm trying to sing songs for women, to say for them what they can't say for themselves. . . . Women today are more independent. They're not slapped around as much. They don't take it as much as they used to. I want to be those women's friend. Like I was a woman whose husband was cheatin' on me, or who worked nine to five, sick to death of my job, sick to death of the kids, sick to death of my husband, sick to death of what I'm havin' to go through—that's the kind of songs I pick. There's a lot of women out there who just want to have three minutes of rebellion.

—REBA McENTIRE, 1993

I'm divorced and I've been to the circus and I've seen the clowns. This ain't my first rodeo.
—NAOMI JUDD, responding to men who have mistaken her for a hillbilly bimbo, 1993

Women don't set out to fall in love with the school bully.

—MARTINA McBRIDE, on battered women, 1995

There's plenty of songs about how women should stand by their men and give them plenty of loving when they walk through the door, and that's fine. But what about the man's responsibility? I feel there's better ways to handle a woman than whippin' her into line. And I make that point clear in my songs. I'm not a big fan of Women's Liberation, but maybe it will help women stand up for the respect they're due.

—LORETTA LYNN, 1993

I was confused by the reaction I got. There's nothing in that song that says to take any kind of abuse. Nowhere in that song does it say, "Be a doormat." It simply says, "If you love him, you'll forgive him."

—TAMMY WYNETTE, defending her song, "Stand by Your Man," 1993

I'm not sitting here, some little woman standing by her man like Tammy Wynette. I'm sitting here because I love and respect [Bill Clinton] and I honor what we've been through together.

—HILLARY RODHAM CLINTON, voicing her support for her allegedly philandering husband on *60 Minutes*, 1992

[Hillary Clinton's remark shows] obvious insensitivity to all "little women" in the country who stand by their men.

—TAMMY WYNETTE, 1992

To people in the South, especially, when you get to a certain age, if you're not married, something is wrong with you.

—WYNONNA JUDD, 1993

A man's word was God in our home and everywhere down there. In the Deep South where I was born, that's exactly how we lived. They still do.

—TAMMY WYNETTE, 1993

Back [in the old days], women were expected to get married and have children. That's all. Well, I just wasn't made that way.

—ROSE MADDOX, 1993

Men used to be the focus of my life. I was caught up in that southern-woman idea that once you had your man, then your life was figured out. —CARLENE CARTER, 1993

What in the world does [Dan Quayle] know of what it's like to go through pregnancy and have a child with no father for the baby? Who is he to call single mothers tramps? I wanted to grow up, fall in love, get married, have two kids, drive a station wagon, and live in a house with a white picket fence. Every woman in America wants that. It doesn't always happen though. . . . The real trouble with these situations isn't the women having children out of wedlock; it's men with no backbone—like Dan Quayle—who don't understand their plight. —TANYA TUCKER, 1993

They didn't have them pills when I was younger, or I'da been swallowin' 'em like popcorn. —LORETTA LYNN, on birth control, 1976

> I'VE SAID MANY TIMES, I THINK SHE'S
> THE FEMALE HANK WILLIAMS.
> —OWEN BRADLEY, producer, on Loretta Lynn, 1993

Wouldn't it be great to be a woman and be just like Willie Nelson? I've often thought, God, would that be great, to be the first woman out there with wrinkles and not trying to cover it up. —LACY J. DALTON, 1993

[In the early days] there was nobody too brainy, or too sexual, or too edgy. . . . It was the girl next door in a gingham skirt and a little folky guitar. The great people have been people that stepped outside that—like a Dolly [Parton] or an Emmylou [Harris] or a Loretta Lynn. They weren't afraid to say what they were thinking. —PAM TILLIS, 1996

~169

Back when we were just starting out, I was at a dinner, and Emmylou Harris was at the same table. And her date was all over her. . . . He leaned over to say something to her, and she didn't look at him, she just held up one finger. And bam, he was a perfect guy the rest of the night. I enjoy women. —GARTH BROOKS, 1994

Patsy [Cline] was the high-strung type, constantly on guard and ready to show you who was boss. She was, of course! To hear her tell it, anyway. You wouldn't have to tell Patsy anything about this women's lib business. She could've taught them a thing or two. —OWEN BRADLEY, producer, 1993

Nothing men do surprises me. I'm ready for them. I know how to whack below the belt. —PATSY CLINE (1932–1963)

Patsy [Cline] I think opened the door for all the girls. She was really proving to the world, and especially the world of country music, that a *woman* could close the show and that she could sell tickets and that she could sell records. Before that, we'd only been used for window dressing. —LORETTA LYNN, 1993

[PATSY CLINE] DIDN'T OPEN THE DOORS FOR THE LADIES IN COUNTRY MUSIC . . . SHE KICKED THEM DOWN!

—GEORGE HAMILTON IV, 1996

The gals were window dressing to keep the men on the edge of their seat. Patsy [Cline] was the first to make them do more than breathe hot and heavy. Some of the male stars who put together the package shows had other things in mind. They'd audition anything in skirts. If they liked how you harmonized their body, quick as a wink you were at a mike. —DEL WOOD, Grand Ole Opry pianist, 1993

I think Kitty Wells was probably a forerunner of Women's Liberation. Hank Thompson put out a song, "Wild Side of Life," in which he said, "I didn't know God made honky-tonk angels." I think women had enough by then and Kitty Wells came back with [the] song . . . "It Wasn't God Who Made Honky-Tonk Angels."

—MARGARET VAUGHN, singer

I think that the "Wild Side of Life" and its answer ["It Wasn't God Who Made Honky-Tonk Angels"] was really a turning point in country music. . . . Kitty came along and gave a different viewpoint, the woman's viewpoint. And from that point forward, songs reflected both sides of the issue and opened the door for the great female vocalists that came along subsequent to that.

—HANK THOMPSON, 1996

I don't believe a country girl singer should do things in the manner [Dolly's] done them. Like the *Playboy* [cover photo] thing. Do you think Kitty Wells would do that?

—PORTER WAGONER, on his one-time protégée, 1988

Dolly Parton has, perhaps more than anyone, defied the stereotype of the dumb blonde and forced society to look beyond the makeup and the mammary glands, no matter how ample either might be.

—RANDALL RIESE, *Nashville Babylon*, 1988

It's a good thing I was born a woman, or I'd have been a drag queen.

—DOLLY PARTON, 1984

LOVE, MARRIAGE, & SEX

LOVE & MARRIAGE: WALK THROUGH THIS WORLD WITH ME

[**M**arriages] often fail, and the public and press have insatiable curiosity about the details.

—RALPH EMERY, radio personality and host of *Nashville Now*, on show business marriages, 1991

My hat's off to people, first of all, who can stay married and, second of all, who can stay married and stay in this business.

—TRAVIS TRITT, 1994

I don't want to think that because we've chosen lives as entertainers and chosen to be married that we can't have both.

—ROBERT REYNOLDS, of the Mavericks, on his marriage to Trisha Yearwood, 1996

I told [my wife], "Being married to an entertainer is like dog years: for every year of marriage, it must feel like seven."

—GARTH BROOKS, 1996

Women who marry people in music or anything that's suppose to be creative really do take their chances. Their chances would be quite a bit better if they married a dentist or a doctor.

—BOB McDILL, songwriter, 1996

We take time apart. That's the secret of a successful marriage is to take your own time apart.

—JOHNNY CASH, 1996

I've learned to walk out of the room a lot.

—EDDY ARNOLD, on the secret to his successful 45-year marriage, 1996

I learned that to maintain a successful [marriage], you have to work at it daily. And that's very tough to do with the road waiting right outside your door. —TRAVIS TRITT, 1994

He got me into this business. That's enough to kill him for.

—LORETTA LYNN, on her husband, 1993

I didn't just fall in love with the image of Dolly Parton. Hell, I fell in love with that exceptional human being who lives beneath all that bunch of fluffy hair, fluttery eyelashes, and super boobs. And I was a fool to believe she loved me back. —MERLE HAGGARD, 1970

I wrote ["I Will Always Love You"] about my relationship and my leaving Porter Wagoner. That was in the very early '70s, and I was trying to leave his show, and he was suing me and we were having lots of trouble. I was heartbroken, and so was he.

—DOLLY PARTON, 1993

Of course it was very disappointing when we split up. But no one understood that we really had planned it that way. I worked hard on her career to get her prepared for the day she would go out and do her own thing. —PORTER WAGONER, 1996

I gave God a prayer, and He let me find Tanya Tucker.

—GLEN CAMPBELL, during his failing marriage to Sarah Davis Campbell, Mac Davis's ex-wife, 1988

I gave God a prayer, too, and He let Glen find Tanya Tucker.

—SARAH DAVIS CAMPBELL, 1988

I truly love him. I felt kinda bad that he didn't steal me from somebody. Who knows what will happen? Tomorrow I may run off with Mac Davis. —TANYA TUCKER, on Glen Campbell, 1988

I called home to find out from [my wife] Cindy. When the answer machine came on, instead of my voice, it was hers. I knew, then, it was over. —BILLY RAY CYRUS, on realizing his marriage had failed, 1993

They really weren't speaking then. It was bad. Toward the end, [George] Jones wouldn't sing anything the same way twice for Tammy [Wynette], and it was hard for her to phrase with him. . . . They just carried on. It made it miserable to [work with], and I thought, "God, this needs to stop."

—BILLY SHERRILL, producer, on how Jones and Wynette's marital problems affected their work relationship, 1993

Certainly, nothing in country's modern era has been as emotionally powerful as the laments George [Jones] directed towards Tammy [Wynette] during his time of greatest pain, a string of darkly beautiful pearls beginning with "The Grand Tour" in 1974, the year of divorce, and ending with "He Stopped Loving Her Today" in 1980. That was one hell of a torch he carried.

—PATRICK CARR, journalist, 1995

I thought about including a chapter, with a headline reading: "Things I Enjoyed About My Marriage to Skeeter Davis." I was going to leave the pages blank.

—RALPH EMERY, radio personality and host of *Nashville Now*, on writing his autobiography, 1991

My life is richer for having spent time with her. It was a good day, but that day is done. That day is over.

—RODNEY CROWELL, on Rosanne Cash, 1994

THE BIGGEST CAUSE OF DIVORCE IN THE WORLD IS MARRIAGE.
—TRAVIS TRITT, 1994

I don't believe in staying married any longer than you stay in love.

—TAMMY WYNETTE, 1993

Divorces, split-ups, extra boyfriends and girlfriends: I don't know where people find the time.

—LORETTA LYNN, 1994

YOU DANCE WITH THE ONE THAT BRUNG YOU [TO THE DANCE].

—GEORGE STRAIT, on fidelity in marriage, 1995

I'm not telling anybody, "If you're not happy, go out and screw around because your wife will become a dynamo for you." [But] I got to be honest with you, that's what happened for me.

—GARTH BROOKS, 1993

I had to deal with that early. Texas girls broke me in, and I just kind of understood that I had to share him with the world.

—JESSI COLTER, wife of Waylon Jennings, on jealousy, 1996

It's hard to live up to what she thinks I can do. I've tried to tell her I ain't as much as she thinks I am.

—WAYLON JENNINGS, on his wife, Jessi Colter, 1975

When you're young and have a guitar and are playing for dances and all those young girls come after you, and you drink a lot, you are going to do things that your wife is not going to like.

—WILLIE NELSON, 1988

When [my wife, Sandy] gets mad, she counts to herself. One night this little gal was drunk and singing on the microphone, trying to get as close to me as she could, and I looked out there and Sandy was on three. I thought, "Oh, God." She didn't even get to five, she just stood up, and grabbed her by the shoulders and threw her off the front of the stage and over the first table.   —GARTH BROOKS, 1993

There was always some girl wanting to put her hand in [Lefty Frizzell's] hair. [His wife, Alice] was very, very high tempered, and very strong. She would whip them girls, and if [he] didn't like it, she'd whip him, too.   —DAVID FRIZZELL, Lefty Frizzell's brother, 1996

I think you ought to stand by your man if he's standin' by you. If he ain't standin' by you, why, move over! I think if your man's doin' you right, fantastic. But how many men treat their wives right? Think about it.

—JEANNE C. RILEY, 1993

Because, they don't give me no shit!

—CARLENE CARTER, on why she named her pickers the Better-Than-a-Husband Band, 1993

Marriage is an institution that some men fear to enter, but a lot of men don't know what fear *is* until they enter it.

—KATIE HAAS, comic, 1996

We all make mistakes. I got married when I was 17. You can't top that one.

—NAOMI JUDD, 1993

You got married [young] either because you're stupid or you're pregnant. . . . Unfortunately, I was both.

—CARLENE CARTER, 1993

First time [I married] I was [18], and I thought she was pregnant. We got married at three P.M. and at eight we found out she wasn't.

—WAYLON JENNINGS, 1975

When you couldn't live at home anymore, you got married, had a passel of kids, got a job down at this or that factory, and spent the rest of your life trying to figure out what went wrong.

—TRAVIS TRITT, on the typical progression of life in rural Georgia, 1994

I had been a confirmed bachelor. I enjoyed being alone, but not lonely.

—BILLY DEAN, on life before marriage, 1993

People reach a certain age and they give up on love, and they get so afraid of being alone the rest of their lives, or whatever it is we're afraid of, and they settle for someone who's wrong for them. I did it.

—LORRIE MORGAN, 1995

Women have always loved me and I've always loved them and gotten along real well with them . . . until I married them.

—WILLIE NELSON, 1988

When I began to realize I might never get married, I thought maybe I didn't need it. In a sense, I know it's better for me not to be married. . . . I wouldn't have any desire to be a traditional wife, and frankly, I don't know what man would want to put up with me.

—LINDA RONSTADT

I'd be in a relationship for three years, tops, because at that point you probably have to get married or break up, and I sure as heck wasn't going to get married.

—WYNONNA JUDD, 1996

Getting married is very special. I only want to do it once. Getting married is like—it's like meeting Elvis.

—TANYA TUCKER, 1980

Falling in love isn't my big problem. Staying in love is. I don't know if I'll ever be married.

—TANYA TUCKER, 1993

I've never been in a happy relationship. My dream—what I've been searching for—is to find a relationship I could be in and still feel creative. I think that's a dilemma for any creative person.

—LUCINDA WILLIAMS, 1993

I need a guy who's happy to sit back while I shine, knowing I'll be back when it's lovin' time. It just messes you up when you have a boyfriend who doesn't understand.

—TANYA TUCKER, 1996

I think everyone has been in love and lost love. At times you do feel like your dreams of that person are reduced to ash. But, hopefully, you sift through those ashes. You take the good, and the lessons learned, with you.

—STEPHANIE BENTLEY, 1996

All you can do is be honest about being vulnerable to love.

—WYNONNA JUDD, 1996

I still really believe my knight in shining armor will come around. If I didn't, I don't know if I could exist. I'm still very much a woman, and some ways a little girl. I like being rocked and held, and . . . to feel safe. I want romance in my life. . . . Maybe I just want a fairy tale.

—LORRIE MORGAN, 1995

I don't know about everybody, but most girls look for a guy like their daddy.

—TANYA TUCKER, 1981

There's a balance now, that there wasn't before. I mean, I'm very career driven. I'm very independent. And I think those are great qualities to have, but if that's all you are . . . something is missing.

—TRISHA YEARWOOD, on finding time for love, 1996

I've heard a lot of entertainers say you have all the loving in the world when you walk out on that stage and you feel the beat of that applause. But, hell, when you leave that stage and the spotlight goes off, that goddamn applause don't help any when you're laying in that bed being ignored. No hit record's worth that.

—DEL WOOD, Opry pianist, 1993

I was lucky enough to find out—and maybe I'm a little slow in learning—that love's the most important thing there is.

—WAYLON JENNINGS, 1994

> ## IT SURE IS A GREAT FEELING THAT SOMEBODY LOVES YOU A LOT AND IS WAITIN' AT HOME FOR YOU.
> —TRACY LAWRENCE, 1995

People in their 40s and 50s have children, and they are very content. But, looking back on those early years when there was that immediate passion—that first time . . . in the end they realize they were so lucky to have felt that way, because some never do.

—PATTY LOVELESS, 1996

I played a party, a dance at [a] ranch out in Oklahoma. She got up on the stage and sang "Redneck Mother." It was really bad . . . but the view was good.

—RONNIE DUNN, of Brooks & Dunn, on how he met his wife, 1995

[His marriage proposal] wasn't one of those tender, romantic things. It was sort of like, "Hey, baby, how 'bout it?" It was so Ronnie Dunn.   —JANINE DUNN, 1996

She was a full-blooded Cherokee and every night with us was like Custer's last stand. . . . I came home drunk [once] and while I was passed out, she sewed me up in a sheet.

—WILLIE NELSON, on his first wife, 1980

One story everybody thinks they know about Willie and me is the one about me catching him passed-out drunk and sewing him up in a bedsheet and then beating the hell out of him with a broom handle. . . . How dumb would I have to be to try to sew Willie into a bedsheet? You know how long that would take to sit there and take stitch after stitch? The truth is, I tied him up with the kids' jump rope before I beat the hell out of him.

—MARTHA JEWEL MATHEWS, Willie Nelson's first wife, 1988

There was only one actual fight [where] I smacked the hell out of her because she was hysterical one night. But if I'd have hit her a couple of times, she'd of picked up a damned chair or something and let me have it.

—CHARLIE DICK, on his marriage to Patsy Cline, 1993

Sober, I love [Charlie Dick]. He tried to do a lot for Patsy. He loved her and them kids . . . worked like the dickens for Patsy. He'd go around to the record companies and call and write the deejays. But, hot damn, if he's drunk and I see him coming, I'll cross the street to get away from him. He gets so damn belligerent. Charlie would beat Patsy around and chew her out something terrible. He was just a Jekyll and a damn Hyde. —FARON YOUNG (1932–1996), 1996

Every time I saw Patsy and asked her how things were, she'd say, "I'm leaving that no-good bastard!" But she didn't. Maybe her name was most misleading: she wasn't anybody's patsy, with the exception of Charlie. —JIMMY DEAN, 1993

[Patsy'd] explode [in the studio], "Get the fuck outa here. You're just in everybody's goddamn way. I don't need you here. You're nothing but a tax write-off." [Charlie'd] be waiting for her when she got home and they'd run into each other's arms. Figure it out! Beats the shit outa me. —FARON YOUNG (1932–1996), 1993

When I met Charlie [Dick] at the Opry that weekend, I wondered if ole Patsy had a bag over her head. I couldn't stand him. I don't know what on earth attracted her to him. They really seemed mad about each other, and love is love. If it's blind, we don't know it till later. —DEL WOOD, Opry pianist, 1993

After we had kids of our own, Doo would take a belt to me as quick as he would to one of them. It's funny how it's the old hurts that never heal. —LORETTA LYNN, on her marriage to Doolittle Lynn, 1993

I had to leave; I actually got run off. It's the hardest thing I've ever done, just to make up my mind and leave. I had circles under my eyes, and I was so nervous. In fact, I was scared to death. You know, you live like that for years, it's hard to get over it, I guess. —LEONA WILLIAMS, on her abusive marriage to Merle Haggard, 1993

He was, from the beginning, the unchallenged head of our household. . . . Any man I could override wouldn't hold my interest for long. —MINNIE PEARL (1912–1996), on her husband, Henry Cannon

[Hank] was in love with [his wife] Audrey, so strong till he couldn't give her up, and he couldn't live with her. She'd try to push him around, to do somethin' he didn't want to do. And, you know, a woman can control a man if she'll just use the right angle. But don't try to push him too far, 'cause he is suppose to be the head of the family.   —NEIL McCORMICK, musician and mentor to Hank Williams, 1996

It was hard for him to express himself. I mean he couldn't just come right out and say [what he was feeling]. But he could write them . . . in his songs.   —MARIZONA ROBBINS, wife of Marty Robbins, 1995

I stink at telling my wife exactly how I feel. I stink at being there for my wife and listening when she talks.   —GARTH BROOKS, 1994

I'm a very indirect person. It's been said by various females that I've been involved with that I'm indirect to the point of dispassion. Not unpassionate, but emotionally, I can be a very solitary person.
    —DWIGHT YOAKAM, 1996

[I am] incredibly disappointed that I still have to see photos in the press of such an unimportant relationship.
    —SHARON STONE, actress, on her affair with Dwight Yoakam, 1993

He's very romantic. People don't know that because he does have a real tough-guy exterior. But he's a real softy.
    —THEA TIPPIN, on her husband, Aaron Tippin, 1996

He told me one time, "I love you so many ways, so many different ways, that you'll *have* to like one of them."
    —DEE HENRY JENKINS, Conway Twitty's widow, 1996

I think a sweetheart is harder to lose than anything. I've put away my mother, my father, my brother. It was hard. But when you lay your sweetheart away . . . that's just almost . . . you can't bear it.
    —ROY ACUFF (1903–1992) on the death of his wife, Mildred

If Keith walked through that door right now, what would we do? Would we be shy, or would we start right in where we left off and end up making love on the kitchen floor?
    —LORRIE MORGAN, on her late husband, Keith Whitley, 1994

She never gave up. I [see] black-white, yes-no, right-wrong, but she can see both sides. If she thought the same way I did, she'd have run me off a long time ago.

—WAYLON JENNINGS on his wife, Jessi Colter, 1994

I don't know if I would have stayed if the shoe was on the other foot. Yeah, I do know. I would not have stayed if the shoe was on the other foot.

—GARTH BROOKS, on his wife, Sandy, forgiving him for his infidelities, 1994

When Arch and I had Elijah, I saw the way he loved our baby. It thrilled my soul to watch them together. He's the greatest father in the world. I got a lot of flack for waiting [to marry], but I didn't want to walk down that aisle until I knew there was no doubt in my mind.

—WYNONNA JUDD, 1996

When the lights go down, you've got to go home and there's got to be somebody waiting there for you who cares. Henry [my husband] has this wonderful gift of bringing me down off the stage. Without being cruel or rude about it, he puts me back in the normal life.

—MINNIE PEARL (1912–1996)

WHEN GOD MADE MINNIE [PEARL], HE MUST HAVE JUST SAT BACK AND BUFFED HIS NAILS.

—HENRY CANNON, 1996

He don't give a damn for show business or this Dolly Parton business. . . . He's got tremendous pride and integrity. Carl and I are very independent people. We don't want to own each other and change things that made us fall in love in the first place.

—DOLLY PARTON on her husband, Carl Dean, 1993

~185

My respect for my wife went up six bazillion notches. I used to think my wife was a puss. But, my God, I could never even think about going through [childbirth]. If it'd been me who had the baby, I'd still be lying there today. —GARTH BROOKS, 1994

He's the best thing that ever happened to me. I'd walk away from all of this music stuff for him in a second. And the thing is . . . he'd never ask me to. —KATHY MATTEA, on her husband, Jon Vezner, 1996

I thought, "This guy's too good to be true. He's gotta be an ax murderer and I just don't know it yet."

—TRISHA YEARWOOD, on first impressions of her husband,
Robert Reynolds of the Mavericks, 1996

We're a pretty hot couple. Every once in a while she tells me, "I ain't gonna be married to no old man," and I tell her the same thing.

—WAYLON JENNINGS, on his marriage to Jessi Colter, 1994

I'M MARRIED, BUT [MY HUSBAND] CARL LETS ME BE SINGLE.
—DOLLY PARTON, 1996

I married [my wife] when she was too young to know any better.
—ALAN JACKSON, 1996

I'm a married man; I've got a young wife. Her baby pictures are in color! —KILLER BEAZ, comic, 1996

SEX: I ALWAYS GET LUCKY WITH YOU

I have a healthy attitude about sex, about the body. . . . I want to be doing it when I'm 83. It's part of life. If God made anything better, he kept if for Himself.

—DOTTIE WEST (1932–1991)

I want to be an 80-year-old lady whose sex life they're still wonderin' about.

—DOLLY PARTON, 1993

A lot of guys thought [Patsy Cline] was the sexiest thing they'd ever seen. I could never see it. . . . Patsy was totally devoid of sex appeal. Still, I loved her to death. There was just no physical attraction. We became the closest of friends. I was already married, so she didn't have an affair with me. I might have been one of the few.

—JIMMY DEAN, 1993

Even when [Patsy Cline] wasn't at her prettiest, I was attracted to her. Patsy's body made up for the rest on those occasions. She was built like a brick shithouse. When she moved, the earth shaked. I couldn't take my eyes off her body. Ah, she had a figure like an hourglass. And what an ass. . . . Oh, she knew what I was thinking. There wasn't no doubt about what I was up to.

—FARON YOUNG (1932–1996), 1993

I'd known Patsy [Cline] a long time and was quite attracted to her. There was an affinity between her and me. We enjoyed each other's company and, after a while, one thing led to another. It was beautiful and special. . . . In each other's arms, it made a few lonely nights on the dismal road more bearable.   —PORTER WAGONER, 1993

[Charlie Dick] satisfies all my wanton desires. Yes, ma'am, there's quite a bit of life in my man. Charlie's bigger than life and twice as hard. —PATSY CLINE, on her husband

A lot of people thought, "Oh, God, there's somethin' goin' on. Gotta be somethin' goin' on." . . . Some of them would think we was cheatin' together. But you don't mess in your own nest. You know? Especially when you're in business. And me and Conway, we're in business together. And even though I love him and he's my friend, I just never felt that.
—LORETTA LYNN, on rumors about her relationship with Conway Twitty, 1988

I'm 40, and all [my generation's] problems with sex, we could cure with a shot. Well, [young people] can't. And the fun times that we thought was the most exciting thing in the world, that's life-threatening to them. My heart goes out to them. But something's gotta jerk their chain and say, "You gotta stop bein' so promiscuous."
—REBA McENTIRE, on AIDS, 1995

I think the reason "Back Street Affair" hit is that there were a lot of people having back street affairs, and it was something they were keeping hidden. . . . They hear somebody singing about back street affairs, they kind of smile and say, "That's us, honey, let's play that one. Let's buy that one." There were enough people saying "That's us, honey" that it sold a lot of records and got a lot of plays.
—WEBB PIERCE, 1996

I'm really at this point where friendship is my most valuable commodity. If I can find somebody that can just have a conversation with me about the ozone layer or about Somalia or about the life of Thomas Edison, or anything, that's very valuable to me. I'm takin' time these days to read people's vibes.
—BILLY RAY CYRUS, on ending his casual affairs, 1993

I don't think I ever had a "cherry." If I did, it got shoved so far back I was usin' it for a taillight.
—DOLLY PARTON

I did some carrying on and chasing in the good old days—I was good for at least eight minutes. —KENNY ROGERS, 1980

I got me a king-size brass bed, and I just had a mirror put up over it—for the exercise. —DOTTIE WEST (1932–1991), 1988

DON'T TRUST LUST.

—PAUL OVERSTREET

Chances are if you're listening to a love song in a saloon and you catch eyes with a woman and think you'd like to take her to bed, she is thinking the same thing about you. —WILLIE NELSON, 1988

Older men have been chasing young girls for years, so it should be okay for women to be involved with younger guys. Why should I go around with some old fuddy-duddy if I don't want to? I'm attracted to younger men, and I'm not afraid to admit it.

—DOTTIE WEST (1932–1991)

I never sold myself out. I never went to bed with anybody unless I wanted to, never for business reasons. —DOLLY PARTON, 1993

The robber said, "Gimmie your money." I said, "But I don't have any money," so he frisked me and said, "Are you sure you ain't got no money?" I said, "Nosir, but if you'll do that again I'll write you a check!" —MINNIE PEARL (1912–1996), telling one of her favorite jokes, 1993

When you make love, your body actually emits a hormone that will drift down the hall, into your child's room and make them want a drink of water. . . . That's what they call a real show stopper.

—JEFF FOXWORTHY, comic, 1996

FAMILY ALBUM

9

MAMA'S HUNGRY EYES

A lot of ignorant people are in the spotlight, and they say traditional family values are a father, mother, 2.3 children, June and Ward out on the lawn. That's bullshit. Traditional family values are happiness and laughing your ass off with your children [even if] your parents are two people of the same sex. As long as those children are happy and they're providing input into this world, that's what traditional family values are.

—GARTH BROOKS, a gay rights supporter, 1993

You can't get rid of your roots. It's either a yoke around your neck, or a wreath around your head. —BRENDA LEE, 1988

Music was a big part of both sides of my family. It was the real escape valve. They worked hard all week long, and the way they celebrated in life was by making music on the weekends. And the music was country music. —RODNEY CROWELL, 1988

My father and my uncle taught me how to play guitar. My grandfather taught them, so it's been handed down. So many people in my family sing, and we just made good music together. I just decided to take it a little further than the living room.

—CLAY WALKER, 1995

One of the most vivid memories of my life is when [my grandfather] would take me out in the fields with him . . . and he would crack a string bean . . . and he would say, "The land is hard, this is a hard life." Even though I got my musical ability from him, he would try to discourage me. "No, no, get a job," he would say. "It's a hard life."

[But late one night, I was teaching myself a Beatles song on my guitar]. I heard my grandfather say to my grandmother upstairs, "You hear that? He's figured it out."   —ED PETTERSEN, singer-songwriter, 1996

Daddy taught me the only three [guitar] chords he knew. Hell, back then that's all you needed to know. That's all country music was.
—MARK CHESNUTT, 1996

[Mama] could sing. Her voice was like pure snow. Dad on the other hand, if he couldn't kick it into place, if he couldn't push it into place, if he couldn't knock it into place . . . there was no reason for doing it.   —DAVID FRIZZELL, Lefty Frizzell's brother, 1996

God put me on this earth to sing. Basically, He gave the voice to Mama. But Mama couldn't use it, so she passed it down to us kids.
—REBA McENTIRE, 1988

Mama sings real good. She's the one that taught us all. I'm gonna do an album sometime called *Songs My Mama Taught Me*. Mama always sang those old songs, those cryin', hurtin' songs. . . . I have such a feelin' for those songs, "Little Rosewood Casket" and all of those old-time numbers.   —DOLLY PARTON, 1993

She'd be cookin' dinner, and she would have a fiddle laying on the bed, and she'd go by the bed and pick it up and play, maybe one number, then go on in the kitchen and do some more cookin'. And she could sing. She had a good voice. And her hair was red. It had just a little bit of light in it. It came way down her back. And she had blue eyes.   —BILL MONROE (1911–1996), on his mother, 1988

I'd love to be able to sing like my granny. You'd hear her and you'd just kind of lift up and float away.   —DWIGHT YOAKAM, 1995

My daddy's mother, my grandmother, was an inspiration to me. She was four foot eleven, weighed about 105 pounds, and had nine kids. On her eighty-fifth birthday she went bowlin' and bowled 168.
—TAMMY WYNETTE, 1993

I just remember Grandma always having a fantastic sense of humor. She taught me how to do some of my favorite things—how to fish, how to bowl, how to play poker, and how to play the guitar.

—CARLENE CARTER, 1993

My mother's a little embarrassed to admit it, but she likes to eat squirrel brains. But back home, it's a real delicacy. You put the head in a pot of boilin' water and crack it open with a spoon.

—DWIGHT YOAKAM, 1995

I think I've had the good fortune of being instilled with a lot of my mother's philosophy. I'm a man, so I don't see things from a feminine perspective. But a lot of my beliefs are based on what my mother felt and what she perceived. I do think I'm a gentleman, and I do hope there's a certain dignity to what I do.

—HAL KETCHUM, 1996

I'll never forget, Jerry Lee Lewis said one time, I think from the most sincere spot down in his soul, . . . he stopped the piano and said, "If I could spend five minutes with my mother, it would straighten out everything that's wrong with me. If I could hear her voice one more time." And boy, I've never wanted to loan [anybody] my mama so bad.

—MARTY STUART, 1996

> I HAVE GREAT MEMORIES OF MY MOM
> WHIPPING UP HER FAMOUS BISCUITS
> WHILE DOLING OUT BITS OF WISDOM. I
> DEEMED HER BISCUITS *MYSTIC*.
> —PAM TILLIS, 1996

[The kitchen] isn't just the heart of our home, this is also where we have what I call "the Pow-Wow." . . . This is where we have our therapy sessions. This isn't just eating, or finding out what each other's lives or thoughts are like. This is where we grow.

—NAOMI JUDD, 1996

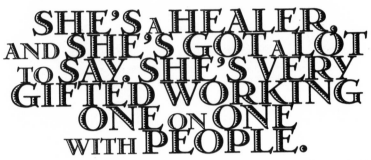

SHE'S A HEALER, AND SHE'S GOT A LOT TO SAY. SHE'S VERY GIFTED WORKING ONE ON ONE WITH PEOPLE.

—ASHLEY JUDD, actress, on her mother, Naomi, 1996

There's a lot of sadness and darkness in my life, but yet I see the light. If it wasn't for Mom . . . surrounding me with unconditional love, I would have gone off the deep end and probably turned into the biggest alcoholic or druggie in the world.

—WYNONNA JUDD, on her mother, Naomi, 1993

I probably know my mother better than anybody. We're just so damned vulnerable to each other. . . . She thought she was right, and I thought I was right. We didn't speak for years. And there was this void in my life, this real black hole. . . . No matter what small victories I had in my life, I still knew something was missing. One of the greatest things I learned, though, is it's not going to happen with [Wynonna and Ashley]. I'm not going to allow that pride, or whatever the heck it was, to happen with them. I've learned that I'd rather be with them and be happy, than be [without them and] be right.

—NAOMI JUDD, 1996

When people meet [me], Marty Stuart's mother, they immediately think of Marty being onstage with all the glitter and the black hair, referred to as "the rooster hair" sometimes. . . . I don't have black hair. I don't have on rhinestones. And I'm not flashy. So sometimes they take a second look. But I try to make them like me anyway.

—HILDA STUART, 1996

Yes, I'm a card-carrying "mama's boy." I love my mama. I think it's good to have a best friend on Earth, and I think you're lucky if that happens to be your mama.   —MARTY STUART, 1996

Just simple things that you miss . . . like smokin' Camels with [my daddy] on the front porch. I was doin' that when I was nine. It was real lonely at home [after Daddy died]. My brother and sister were gone, and I was by myself, and I felt like a real burden to Mom. So I ran away.   —MERLE HAGGARD, 1989

I was torn between two things, you know. I had this family over here, the staunch, religious side, the Baptists . . . my mother. Then I had my dad over here, the complete epitome of the all-American hell-raiser. I had to make the choice myself. I tried the complete religious side for a while, and finally made up my mind to take the middle road: music.

—RONNIE DUNN, of Brooks & Dunn, on going from the ministry to music, 1995

[In public] I'm representing my father's name and my mother's name and I don't want anything to get back to them. I was afraid my dad would spank my butt as a kid. And the bigger fear was breaking my mom's heart.   —GARTH BROOKS, 1994

I could have turned out a lot worse but I have too much respect for my family.   —TANYA TUCKER, 1980

With the first money I got, I built my parents a house back home, gave them a string of credit cards, and said, "Go!"

—GLEN CAMPBELL, 1980

My mom and dad, as I was growing up . . . would say, "Do this or do that," or "Don't do this or don't do that." And I would ask,

"Why?" They would answer with "Because I said so." That's not right. . . . If you don't have a good answer to a "Why?" then you shouldn't have the right to give the order to begin with.

—WAYLON JENNINGS, 1994

Back then, there's no doubt that I was haunted by Daddy. I'd sit in front of a record player, play Daddy's records, get the biggest bottle of Jim Beam I could find, and try to communicate with him.

—HANK WILLIAMS, JR., 1988

I don't know if I was running from something or running to it, but I was really trying to get from underneath [Mel Tillis's] shadow. I had an identity crisis. And so I thought maybe if I did another type of music, I could assert myself and carve out a niche, a place for myself. It turns out I didn't have to go that far.

—PAM TILLIS, Mel Tillis's daughter, 1996

His audience on the farm was in the field, out in front of his balcony, full of cattle. And he'd go out there in the middle of the night, play his guitar and sing. And I would sneak out, crawl under him, and listen to him sing. He was touched by that.

—JANET ROBBINS, Marty Robbins's daughter, 1995

It was a part of my life, through the week, just watching my dad rehearse. I saw my dad be at the bottom, I mean, when he didn't have nothin' and the whole world was on his shoulders. Just gettin' on a little stage with a guitar . . . seemed like the only time I seen him smile.

—JOHN MICHAEL MONTGOMERY, 1996

He was a good man, he was a good farmer, and he raised eight children. And you stayed with him and worked there till you's 21, then you went out on your own. And when you become 21 years old, he would give you 100 dollars, or he would give you a new horse. That's the way he raised all of his children.

—BILL MONROE (1911–1996), on his father, 1988

Dad was the greatest man I'll ever know—and he never really succeeded in any type of business. Every time he got into something, it seemed like it went wrong . . . but he was the most successful man I've ever known. —WAYLON JENNINGS, 1974

The guy you call Father is just a kid himself in his own mind. Maybe he's got some gray hairs and his face is wrinkled like a road map, but inside he is wondering how it can be that the mirror tells him he ain't young anymore. The face he sees in the mirror changes from being a little kid or a teenager into being a grown-up and then an elderly person so fast it seems impossible. . . . It's certainly tough for a kid to understand that the guy they call Father who is out there screwing up right and left is really just doing the best he can. . . . Go hug your daddy. It ain't too late to save him.
—WILLIE NELSON, 1988

Daddy was a hard worker and well built, a good fellow, except when he was drinkin'. But three beers and he was a crazy man. . . . [Me and my siblings] used to be punished with rice. You ever try to kneel on rice for an hour? It doesn't seem like much, but it sure hurts. —SAMMY KERSHAW, on his father's alcohol-fueled abuse, 1994

[My family and I] had our problems. Daddy, he often ran around, and he had some children outside of us. But he was a good father and a good husband. He always came home. He was just a little wild. —DOLLY PARTON, 1993

You know, when I was a kid that was all I wanted to do was run barrels and be the world champion barrel racer. And Daddy always told me, "Reba, go do somethin' you *can* do, honey."
—REBA McENTIRE, on her rodeo days, 1995

I will never forget the big words of wisdom my father gave me about my desire to be an entertainer: "Son, it won't surprise me if you make it, but it would surprise me if you didn't."
—BILLY DEAN, 1996

The thing about writing your autobiography is that you go back. It's almost like reliving everything. You go back to where your grandparents lived and somehow, you think they're gonna still be there . . . and they're not. —WAYLON JENNINGS, 1996

The thing that strikes me the hardest about those days [touring with Lester Flatt at such a young age] was when my mom, dad, and sister, Jennifer, came down to Jackson, Alabama, to talk to Lester, to meet him. . . . [My parent's] car drove out in front of the [tour] bus, that red dirt just flying. When we got to the end of that road, my mom and dad and sister's car took a left, and we took a right. I watched their car as far as I could see it go. That was kind of a lonesome moment. I knew it was the crossroads.
—MARTY STUART, 1996

The things that I would have died for, that I would have traded my family for, are so unimportant. The things I thought were the bust-ass important things aren't. Bein' a dad seems to be a pretty full-time job. If you came up and said you were going to burn my barn and take all my horses, I'd say, "Just don't take my daughter."
—GARTH BROOKS, 1993

WHEN YOU'RE NUMBER ONE FOR FIVE
MINUTES AND THEN GO HOME
AND CHANGE A DIAPER, IT PUTS
IT ALL IN PERSPECTIVE.
—WYNONNA JUDD, on being a new mother, 1996

I consider myself a major contribution toward wreckin' my family, and I want [my daughter, Charlotte] to know that I was wrong, and that I haven't forgotten that. I try not to forget the mistakes I've made, or to side-step 'em or deny 'em. —AARON TIPPIN, 1994

Lately, I find myself thinking a lot about starting a family. Yet, I know I'm not in the right place in my life. I don't want to sound like some 30-something yuppie casualty, but I do wonder sometimes if it will ever be the right time. I wonder if I'm too demanding in terms of what it would take for me to feel secure enough.

—MARY CHAPIN CARPENTER, 1993

I love the age my children are at right now: five and seven. I just signed 'em up for soccer, and I looked at my schedule, and I'm going to be home for one game. I just get real emotional about that stuff. All their growin' up while I'm away just tears me up.

—KIX BROOKS, of Brooks & Dunn, 1994

I have a daughter, and she's 12 now. Pretty soon these hairy-legged boys are gonna be showin' up. One's gonna run off with her someday and break my heart.

—VINCE GILL, 1995

She's beautiful. She loads my .44 Magnum right with me.

—HANK WILLIAMS, JR., on quality time with his daughter, 1996

You know, I've been down that same road she has, it's just something I can relate to and love her more for, because she's overcome [drugs]. I wasn't smart enough to do it that young. I admire her very much. And her songwriting too. She wrote a great song about me called "My Old Man."

—JOHNNY CASH, on his daughter, Rosanne, 1996

I'm proud of my son, because he never runs from his responsibilities. It's always been our belief that you don't measure a person by how they hold up in good times, but in bad.

—RUTH ANN ADKINS, Billy Ray Cyrus's mother, 1993

My [new] daughter is just beautiful. She is the prettiest thing I've ever seen. She has some great lungs that will come in handy should Little Texas ever need a female singer.

—TIM RUSHLOW, of Little Texas, 1996

People always ask, do you give your daughter advice? No, I ask her advice.

—JOHNNY CASH, on his daughter, Rosanne, 1994

WE NICKNAMED HIM SHOOTER BECAUSE HIS DADDY WAS SUCH A PISTOL.

—WAYLON JENNINGS, on his son, Albright Jennings, 1979

[Me and my son, Shooter] was coming out of a store. This woman said, "Oh, you must be Shooter." He said, "Yeah." She said, "You gonna grow up to be just like your daddy?" He said, "No!" Well, that hurt my feelings. . . . I said, "Shooter, what'd I do? Am I doin' somethin' wrong? You don't want to be like me?" He said, "No, Dad. I love you. I just don't want to smoke and I don't want to sing."

—WAYLON JENNINGS, 1996

I was scared to death. I didn't think I'd be a good father and I didn't think that I really knew what love was enough to take care of a child. I knew there was no way I could be the dad my dad was to me. But when that kid came, it was like the instructions came with her and they were just "Love me." And, whew, that's cool.

—GARTH BROOKS, 1994

I think I'm the only man in captivity whose daughter screams at him, "Turn that thing down!"   —VINCE GILL, on blasting his stereo, 1994

All babies are ugly, I think. They've been layin' in a sack of water for nine months!   —T. BUBBA BECHTOL, comic, 1995

I guess nine months was too long for me to stay in [the womb]. I tried to pound my way out.

—KIX BROOKS, of Brooks & Dunn, explaining the origin of his unusual name, 1995

SING ME BACK HOME

I know that what I'm doin' now reflects so much on how I was brought up. . . . That's why I wish that I could raise my kids up in the same kind of atmosphere, gettin' out and gettin' fleas and ticks on 'em, you know. And bein' able to go fishin', walk around in the hills, and go see a coal mine. And bein' able to go out and pick tomatoes off the vine, instead of goin' to a store and gettin' 'em. I didn't know that you could buy tomatoes in a store until I was 15 years old.

—RICKY SKAGGS, 1988

I was home-grown and hand-spanked!   —AL RICE, songwriter, 1996

In the summertime, [all of us kids] would bathe in the creek and the river. And in the wintertime we always just washed with a wash-pan of water. You'd wash down as far as "possible," then you'd wash up as far as "possible." And when your brothers cleared the room, you'd wash *possible*.

—DOLLY PARTON, 1996

I'd [like] to bring back the old times, when life was safe and slow. And people closed the door against the world on a Saturday night, everybody was in, studying their Sunday school lessons, takin' their baths . . . I don't know. It was a safe world, warm, secure.

—MINNIE PEARL (1912–1996)

Everything I know about my childhood, everything I feel about my childhood, was nothing but Disneyland. Great place.

—GARTH BROOKS, 1994

~203

Take my word for it, I was mean. I hated my teenage years. Just one massive conflict. I wallpapered my room with demerits.

—ROSANNE CASH, 1993

HANK THE TANK! DEFENSIVE END, OFFENSIVE END, FULLBACK, RUN BACK, KICK, AND GOIN' WITH THE COACH'S DAUGHTER!

—HANK WILLIAMS, JR., on his high school days, 1996

There's a lot of things I've done wrong in my life and mistakes I've made. And quitting school was the worst. It set up this pattern. Like back in the old westerns with the gunslingers. They said that when you killed one man, the second was easier. Well, when you quit one thing, the second one is easier because you've already established yourself as a quitter.

—WAYLON JENNINGS, 1994

When I was a little kid, I would pick cotton or I would clean a ditch. I wouldn't get but about 25 cents a day, but it only cost 10 cents to get into the movies. I'd go in at 12:45, when it opened, and I'd stay till Gene Autry was through that night. Then I'd walk back across the desert, by myself, just a little kid. But I wasn't scared 'cause I'd just seen Gene Autry . . . and I *was* Gene Autry that night.

—MARTY ROBBINS (1925–1982)

The great white hats are gone. We've got action movies. We have adventure movies. You can upset 28 cars. You can set a whole town on fire. But you don't have the heroes. You don't have the guy in the white hat that steps on that horse with that silver saddle. And you look at him and say, "Man, I want to be like that." We don't have that anymore.

—HAROLD REID, of the Statler Brothers, 1996

I didn't like pickin' cotton one bit, and so I'd often end up day-dreaming. I used to stand in the fields and watch the cars go by and think, "I want to go with *them*." —WILLIE NELSON, 1993

I may not have been the best singer in church, but boy I was the loudest. And the quartets were just so distinguished looking. And the women wore frilly chiffon dresses, stuff that I'd never seen before, never had. And I wanted to be part of that so bad.
—TAMMY WYNETTE, 1993

I was thinkin' I was gonna be a star. I thought I was singin' to a lot of people when I was singin' to my brothers and sisters and the chickens and the dogs with a tin can as a make-believe microphone.
—DOLLY PARTON, 1993

The curling iron was a great microphone, because it had a cord, you know, and that's better than using a hairbrush.
—TRISHA YEARWOOD, on performing in front of the mirror as a child, 1996

We had a tree stump in our backyard that I used as a stage. I'd get up on the stump, pretending I was on the Opry, and say, "Hello, this is Porter Wagoner and I'm glad to have you listening in. Tonight my special guest will be Roy Acuff." Then I'd get off the stump, run around and come back up on the other side as Roy Acuff. —PORTER WAGONER, 1996

My parents have an audiotape of me when I was four years old. They were asking us kids, "What do you want to be when you grow up?" I took the microphone and said, "I am going to be a country music star." They still have that tape and I've actually got a copy of it.
—CHELY WRIGHT, 1996

When I was little, I used to play 45s over and over and over to see if I could wear out the singer. I thought every time you played them, they sang the song. I thought I could make Tammy Wynette get tired by playing her single. —JO DEE MESSINA, 1996

THAT BUZZ YOU ALWAYS HEAR IN THE BACKGROUND OF AM RADIO— THAT'S THE SOUND OF MY CHILDHOOD.

—DWIGHT YOAKAM, 1996

I walked out on that stage with my hands stuffed into the pockets of my little black suit, and I sang "Lovesick Blues" in my little eight-year-old voice. The audience loved it. They went crazy shouting about "Hank's little boy." —HANK WILLIAMS, JR., 1993

As I got better, I realized the old Tempo [guitar] was only a notch better than those toy ukuleles with a hand crank on the side that play the Mouseketeer theme. But it was a guitar. And I could play it, thanks to one of those chord books. . . . I was awful.

—TRAVIS TRITT, 1994

There wasn't a damn thing to do out there in West Texas. You know, I think that's why, certainly in Del Rio, I had to learn to make my own fun. —RADNEY FOSTER, on taking up the guitar, 1996

I started writing while driving a tractor for my dad. Out on those West Texas plains, you know, where every direction you looked was over the horizon. —BUTCH HANCOCK, songwriter, 1996

As far back as I can remember, I was intrigued by the guitar. I can remember when I was three, trying to get out of this jumper swing and reaching for my daddy's guitar—an old Gene Autry with a cowboy on a horse rearin' up. —WAYLON JENNINGS, 1984

[We'd] go to a place settin' 10 miles out in the country, a big dance hall, all by itself. It come show time and the Maddox Brothers and

Rose pulled up in them Cadillacs. People's eyes bugged out, their mouths hung open and [they] said, "What is it?"

—ROSE MADDOX, 1996

I don't know why anyone would want to hear about my sordid past, but I'm told a lot of folks do.

—GEORGE JONES, on writing his autobiography, 1996

THE STRUGGLE

One of the greatest gifts a person can have is to be born poor.
                                    —NAOMI JUDD, 1994

I think sometimes having less . . . even a lot less, sometimes makes you a better person.
                    —SHANIA TWAIN, on her impoverished childhood, 1996

I've been through a lot more and a lot harder [times] but it sure did improve my singing.
                                    —DOLLY PARTON, 1982

I growed up poor, without no daddy. I went to high school and graduated with seven other people. I never saw a football till I got to college. And the first college football game I ever saw, I played in. I got my degree in agriculture due to me playing football. So, all of you young'uns out there whining, "You can't do it!" Shut up!
                                    —JERRY CLOWER, comic, 1996

> ## THE PROVERBIAL WOLF AT THE DOOR HAD A LITTER OF PUPS ON MY BACK PORCH.
> —RED FOLEY

Once you've been poor, you always feel in the back of your mind that you'll be poor again.
                                    —LORETTA LYNN, 1994

The heat was turned off, the lights was turned off, and all I had to eat was a can of corn. Only thing I had to open it with was a butter knife, but I guarantee you I got that sucker open!

—MARTY RAYBON, of Shenandoah, 1995

Like most people, we were poor, but we had plenty to eat. Plenty of biscuits and gravy.

—GEORGE JONES, 1988

I remember eatin' offa tin plates as a little girl. And Mommy had these old kegs, barrels that you get nails in and stuff. That's what I'd eat off of, asettin' on the floor.

—LORETTA LYNN, 1993

Back home when you got cold, the best you could do to keep warm was to throw another hound dog in the bed. And if you didn't have a hound dog, you got married.

—TENNESSEE ERNIE FORD (1919–1991)

It's like they say sports is with black dudes. It's a way to get up and away from something that's bad. I tell you what it is: either country music or pull cotton for the rest of your life.

—WAYLON JENNINGS, on country music as a way to escape poverty, 1994

From the time she was about 10, Patsy was living, eating, and sleeping country music. I know she never wanted anything so badly as to be a star on the Grand Ole Opry. . . . Everybody she spoke to about becoming a singer told her how tough it would be for a woman to go into country music. But that didn't faze Patsy. Knowing her, it probably made her all the more determined.

—HILDA HENSLEY, Patsy Cline's mother

I got off the bus with my A-line skirt, my matching luggage, my cat, and my perfect hairdo, and winos start spillin' booze on my shoes. I thought, girl, what have you *done*!

—K. T. OSLIN, on her first impression of New York, 1993

I'm sure every trash can in Nashville has seen one of my [early demo] tapes at one time or another.

—TANYA TUCKER, 1996

I still think a lot of what we called our "Bronco tours," where we'd just climb in our cars and drive around the country to shows and radio interviews, before we could afford to rent a bus. It seems like yesterday, it feels like yesterday.

—MARY CHAPIN CARPENTER, 1995

You [would] call up the owner of a club and tell him you're the greatest act in the history of country music, which he knows is bull, and that, if he should hire you, about 10,000 of your closest friends will be there every night to support you, buying liquor like there's no tomorrow.

—TRAVIS TRITT, on the early days of pitching his act, 1994

I'm very proud. I was the one person who was in these shoes through the whole trip, and I've seen the whole thing go down, from the day I bought the guitar and had a dream and a vision of sitting here talking to you right now. I could give you a big depressing scenario here of . . . the abuses I've went through, but just understanding that I've done this for this long kind of says it. I've been to the fair and seen the bear.

—BILLY RAY CYRUS, 1995

[A Grammy nomination is] a payoff for all the sacrifices . . . and I won't say sufferin', but . . . near sufferin', I've done for the last 20 years of my career. That's what it's about, to be part of the game.

—JUNIOR BROWN, 1995

I JUST ROLLED WITH THE PUNCHES AND GOT VERY, VERY LUCKY.

—LARRY STEWART, on finding success, 1996

You wait all your life for something to happen, and then when you're not even trying . . . it all just fell into place.

—PAM TILLIS, 1995

[Merle Haggard] liked the climb [to success] better than he liked sitting up on top. It seemed like he did everything he could to get knocked down so he could climb back up.

—BONNIE OWENS, Haggard's first wife, 1996

> # ANYTHING WORTH HAVING IS WORTH WORKING FOR AND I'M USED TO SWEATIN'.
> —DOLLY PARTON, 1995

I have been through so much in my life. I've had people die in my arms, I've been divorced, fired, slam-dunked, and shot at. . . . I have crawled over broken glass to get here.   —NAOMI JUDD

I've got a room full of awards now. And as I go back and look at 'em, I know what I achieved to get each one. . . . When young people ask me how I got where I'm at, I say, "It's absolutely hard work." There ain't nobody gonna wave a magic wand. . . . You pay for what success you get.   —LORETTA LYNN

It's true that I had to step over a few people because they was unwilling to budge or move, but I never walked on anybody to get where I'm at.   —DOLLY PARTON, 1981

HOMESPUN
TRUTH &
SPIRITUALITY

LIFE'S A DANCE (YOU LEARN AS YOU GO)

The hardest thing to control in this body is that serpent called the tongue. —GLEN CAMPBELL, 1988

Keep your chin up and your skirt down. —PATSY CLINE (1932–1963)

Just because you want everybody to know you're country doesn't mean you have to act stupid. —ALLEN REYNOLDS, producer, 1996

If you're gonna wear a cowboy hat, you gotta remember a few golden rules. You must never hold the hat by the crown, this is not to be done for any reason. Handle the hat by the brim, and when you're passing another man his hat, hand it to him with the crown down and the back facing yourself, so he can flip it onto his head in one easy motion. You must never put your hat on your bed, 'cause that'll bring bad luck for sure. Put it on the floor next to your bed and never, ever wear another man's hat. Hell! That's almost a whippin' offense. —JIM MacKENZIE, Wyoming rodeo commentator, 1995

Y'all don't worry, 'cause it ain't gonna be all right nohow. —HANK WILLIAMS (1923–1953)

Expel that pain and you'll be free from it, someday, some way. —DWIGHT YOAKAM, 1995

There's a time to hang in there and not let go, but there's also a time to move on, and that's probably the hardest thing we have to do as adults—to learn when to let go. —WYNONNA JUDD, 1996

There'll be a lot of people sayin' no, a lot of things will be frustrating. But hang in there, 'cause cream always rises to the top.
—JOE DIFFIE, 1996

Get rid of [a man] if he starts to mess you up.
—DEL WOOD, Opry pianist, 1993

Don't give any shit, and put up with very little.
—HANK WILLIAMS, JR., 1996

If there was ever any message I was trying to get across to people, it's a simple one. The message is just that no matter what you're trying to do in life, there is another way—*your* way. And everyone, whether it's you or me or anybody, has a right to try it at least once in their life.
—WAYLON JENNINGS, 1985

It's easy to find people who'll tell you what you can't do. Too easy. And it doesn't matter if it's in the guise of, "You stink," or "I'm only telling you this for your own good." The result is the same.
—TRAVIS TRITT, 1994

I think life is an apprenticeship. You can find masters if you just look.
—HAL KETCHUM, 1995

Experience is a hard teacher. She gives the tests first, and the lessons come after.
—PATSY CLINE (1932–1963)

You don't learn about yourself through your successes. You learn through your failures and your mistakes.
—WYNONNA JUDD, 1996

Minnie Pearl told me once how there's a lesson to be learned every night you're onstage. The more you do something, the better you get at it. . . . The second time you make any trip, you know which roads to take and not to take.

—CHELY WRIGHT, 1996

Sometimes Fate walks into our lives wearing the strangest disguises.

—TRAVIS TRITT, 1994

They say a mind is a terrible thing to waste. Well, I say a dream is a terrible thing to waste. And I've always been a dreamer; I was born a dreamer.

—DOLLY PARTON, 1993

We will never stop paying for our sins of the past until we change our thinking about the present and the future.

—WILLIE NELSON, 1988

You can't change yesterday anymore than you can predict what is gonna happen tomorrow.

—GLEN CAMPBELL, 1980

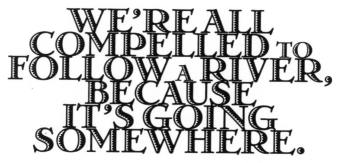

WE'RE ALL COMPELLED TO FOLLOW A RIVER, BECAUSE IT'S GOING SOMEWHERE.

—DWIGHT YOAKAM, 1995

Your body hears everything your mind says.

—NAOMI JUDD, 1994

No matter how handsome you are, how beautiful you are, you're not going to make it without luck.

—TENNESSEE ERNIE FORD (1919–1991)

By being the kind of person you are, by recording the songs you record. By always trying to make it better. Only longevity can help you put more back into it.

—CONWAY TWITTY (1933–1993), on how to stay true to your music

I would say, "Go for it. Just do it. And don't let anybody tell you you can't." It's a long way from Oklahoma and Louisiana and Mississippi up to that ACM [Academy of Country Music] stage, performing or accepting an award. It's a long trip, but it's possible.

—FAITH HILL, her advice to aspiring country western performers, 1996

Keep it slow, keep it steady, build that foundation. Go play music that you love to play with people that you love to play with. That'll feed you, and it also comes in real handy for your soul, down through the years.

—LESTER FLATT'S musical advice to Marty Stuart, 1995

My theory has always been, if you don't go out to be the best there is, why dress up and go out at all? —GARTH BROOKS, 1994

If [your art] is not doing something for you spiritually, then why are you doing it? —MARY CHAPIN CARPENTER, 1993

Remember one thing: mean what you sing and sing what you mean. —ERNEST TUBB (1914–1984)

IF YOU CAN'T DO IT WITH FEELING, DON'T.

—PATSY CLINE (1932–1963)

When Patsy Cline had her car accident, she came to the Opry on crutches and sang, even though she was clearly in pain. Someone said it was great she did that for the fans, and Patsy said, "I didn't do it just for the fans. It was also for me. You don't get anywhere wallerin' in misery." I don't waller. Never have. I believe in gettin' on with things and movin' ahead.

—DOLLY PARTON

I figure there ain't no shame in gettin' knocked down in life, but there is shame in stayin' down.   —HOYT AXTON, 1996

Part of overcoming tough times is having a vision of what you want to achieve.   —TRACY LAWRENCE, 1996

If you look, and it doesn't take much digging, you can find the negative in anything.   —TRAVIS TRITT, 1994

Life is peaks and valleys. It's surviving those valleys that makes the peaks worthwhile.   —BILLY RAY CYRUS, 1996

A 90-year-old woman took [my father] through her house just before she died. And she said to him, "I want to tell you something, and I want you to remember it. Every material possession you acquire becomes a stick to beat you with. Live simply."

—ROSANNE CASH, repeating words of wisdom from her father, Johnny Cash, 1988

My daddy used to say, "You got to chop hay while the sun is shinin'." And that's exactly how I feel.

—MARTY RAYBON, of Shenandoah, 1995

Daddy said, "Son, it's okay to dream, as long as you work your ass off while your dreamin'. So dream on."

—DOUG STONE, 1996

CHASING a DREAM IS ALMOST AS MUCH FUN AS LIVING IT.

—KIX BROOKS, of Brooks & Dunn, 1996

I think you've got to go over the edge, take that dive, do something wacky once in a while. But you can't do it all the time, then it's not an adventure anymore. . . . Someday, I think I'll have bumper stickers made: "Excess in Moderation." It's my motto.

—LARI WHITE, 1996

It's not what happens to you that's really important. It's what you *do* with the things that happen to you.   —WYNONNA JUDD, 1996

Put the dime in the slot yourself. If you're not satisfied with the life, do something about it.   —MEL TILLIS, 1994

You can't get a seven if you don't ever throw the dice.

—HANK WILLIAMS, JR., 1988

We don't deal the cards, we just play the hand. That's just the way it is.   —LORETTA LYNN, 1993

I just try to enjoy life. I mean, who can figure it out anyway?

—DOLLY PARTON, 1996

I'm an example of real life. Life is unpredictable . . . life is messy.

—WYNONNA JUDD, 1996

The only thing in life that's constant is change; you change or you die.   —CONWAY TWITTY (1933–1993)

Not knowing anything is maybe better than just knowing a little.

—WILLIE NELSON, 1980

God respects you when you work, but He loves you when you sing.

— PAM TILLIS, 1996

I'm not really sure that for the past three years anybody's been at the helm of this [career], other than God. Believe me, if there were hands on the wheel, they weren't mine.

— GARTH BROOKS, 1994

The voice told me to pick up a guitar, form a band, and sing. I realized that I wasn't just set here by accident. I was to use my life for something good, for something positive. I felt very strongly at that moment that music was to be my chosen thing.

— BILLY RAY CYRUS, 1993

The fact that we have been so successful makes us think there must be a higher reason for it.

— MARTY RAYBON, of Shenandoah, 1995

I think we keep on goin' till we get it right.

— LORETTA LYNN, on reincarnation, 1993

> ## IF YOU WANT TO MAKE GOD LAUGH, JUST TELL HIM YOUR PLANS.
> — MINNIE PEARL (1912–1996)

No one needs a preacher to tell them they're a sinner. God gave us the ability to know the difference between right and wrong, no matter who we are, or if we ever read the Bible.

—WAYLON JENNINGS, 1994

I no longer believe in religion so much as spirituality, though I do believe there's a place for religion. I think you need ritual to a certain extent to help keep your life on track. —BOBBIE CRYNER, 1994

I think organized religion is in trouble. . . . If you have the church door open and don't make black people feel welcome in a white man's church, that's wrong. I don't want to go to their heaven.

—WAYLON JENNINGS, 1983

I'm a firm believer in Christ; there's not a doubt in my mind. . . . The fact is that Jesus said don't pray out in front, for everybody to see. . . . You don't have to advertise all the time. And I don't think you have to ram it down people's throats. I think people know. I don't believe you have to be in the Assembly of God to go to heaven. —TRAVIS TRITT, 1996

I believe in Jesus. I believe that God is the divine, supreme intelligence behind our universe. But, when you become a fanatic . . . it was fanatics that put Jesus on the cross. . . . Only the ignorant become fanatics. —NAOMI JUDD, 1994

If you really, seriously, in all faith, get quiet and pray and ask Jesus, He will answer you. This is the truth. He won't necessarily set fire to a bush or send a bolt of lightning. Instead the answer will come through your inner voice, your conscience, your divine spirit.

—WILLIE NELSON, 1988

It's a hard life for people sometimes, when they haven't had that good family, that Christian upbringing, you know. And I know that if you raise your kids up with that solid Christian life, they won't ever forget it. It'll always be in the back of their minds.

—RICKY SKAGGS, 1988

There's such a close relationship between the church and music in the South. It's part of the Southern landscape—you sing in the church. It is inspirational. If you don't feel better than you did when you got there, then you probably shouldn't be going to start with. —TRAVIS TRITT, 1994

I went to church by chance one Sunday at Jimmy Snow's. Larry Gatlin was there singing and he sang "Help Me." It moved me in a weird way. It really affected me. It got to be a kind of profound experience and blew my mind wide open. —KRIS KRISTOFFERSON, 1996

[Southerners] raise hell on Saturday night, and we're in church on Sunday mornin'. It's a dichotomy of our being.

—ALICE HAYES, former director of the Hank Williams Museum, Crossville, Tennessee, 1996

"You think you're runnin' free, Jeannie, but you ain't. Like a heifer on a rope, one day you'll take off arunnin' and almost break your neck, because that rope's tied to God's tree."

—JEANNIE C. RILEY, recalling a warning from her mother, 1993

People think you have to give up so much to be a Christian, you know. They think, "Well, I've gotta quit livin' if I do that. I can't drink no more, and I can't get out and gamble and play poker." But the Lord gives you so many things that's so much better than all that. You don't even remember that you done 'em.

—RICKY SKAGGS, 1988

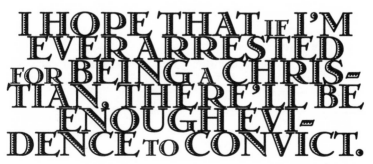

I HOPE THAT IF I'M EVER ARRESTED FOR BEING A CHRISTIAN, THERE'LL BE ENOUGH EVIDENCE TO CONVICT.

—JOHNNY CASH, 1994

I figure she's got a direct line to God, and that leaves me in pretty good shape.   —WAYLON JENNINGS, on his wife, Jessi Colter's, spirituality, 1996

As long as God is with you and you have faith, you have friends who have that intercom system with God, then you shouldn't be afraid.   —MAE BOREN AXTON, songwriter, on using her faith to fight her cancer, 1996

I was having a conversation with a friend, and we began to talk about the world, and the future of the world and the changes that a new century brings. And . . . I found myself feeling a little scared, hollow, empty. You know, that feeling that the unknown and the uncertain brings. But [then] I came across the comforting thought that God sees it all. He knows all about it. Change is nothing new for Him. It's okay.   —MARTY STUART, 1996

I know without a doubt that it's the hand of God that's brought me through a lot of my self-destructive times. I can almost hear Him say, "Not yet, Cash. I'm not through with you yet." He'd straighten me out and slap me.   —JOHNNY CASH, 1994

I thank God that He allowed me to keep a piece of my sanity through this whole 33 years that I've been on this earth.   —BILLY RAY CYRUS, 1995

I thank God that He gave my children a chance to live through that. Twenty minutes before we were hit head-on was the first time we had ever worn seat belts.   —BARBARA MANDRELL, on her 1984 near-fatal car accident, 1995

I don't think God intended for man to fly. It says right there in the Bible, "*Lo,* I am with you always." It don't say nothin' about high.   —RAY STEVENS, on his fear of flying, 1996

MORTALITY

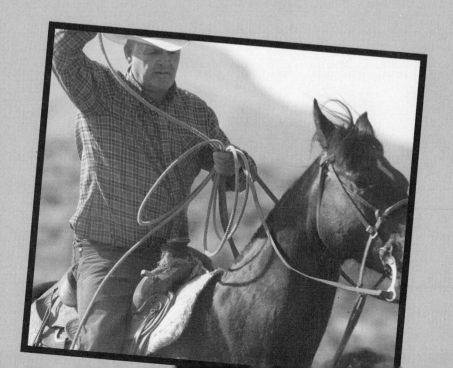

OLD-TIMERS & YOUNG BLOOD

This so-called new country is nothin' but rock stuff for kids to dance by . . . and to hell with the older people that helped country music to get established to start with. They've throwed them to the wolves! —GEORGE JONES, 1995

They say young people are ruining country music—they're turning it into something that doesn't even resemble country music. They're not. It's just *their* way. And I don't criticize them. We've had our day. Now let them have theirs. —MINNIE PEARL (1912–1996), 1988

I don't see anything wrong with what [young country artists are] doing. Seems to me they're making music, trying to have fun and make a little money. Somebody said there's nothing more permanent than change. It's a free country. I think young people should be doing whatever the hell they please. Music is like air: you can get it wherever you want. —TOM T. HALL, 1996

I figure country music needs a few warriors out there [who] knows where it came from to bring it into the twenty-first century. —MARTY STUART, 1994

[All the new country artists] are good—not better. Not better than Merle Haggard or George Jones. —EMMYLOU HARRIS, 1996

I think once you're over 40, you're just [not worth] zip anymore. I've never been able to figure out what age has to do with talent, and [the radio people] don't do that to the rockers—who are in

their late 40s and 50s. Look at Elton John [who's 47]. I don't know what it is about country music that they won't play our records.
—TAMMY WYNETTE, 1995

You don't find many kids that like country music, because they don't really understand the lyric. 'Cause most songs are about cheatin' and hurtin'. They don't understand those kinds of things, because they haven't lived 'em yet. And in country music, you have to live it, I mean it's real. You got to live it to understand it.
—CONWAY TWITTY (1933–1993)

These [new] songs don't really talk about love or the acquisition of it or the loss of it, or what's going on in people's lives. Because kids 18 to 25 haven't lived that. Sooner or later country music has to come back to what country music has always come back to, and that is songs that are the soundtrack of the everyday ordinary working person, songs that mean something to people.
—TRAVIS TRITT, 1996

Once again, I feel like the underdog. It's new blood, a fresh breath. It's like, yeah! I'm back in the fight . . . this is like the old days.
—GARTH BROOKS, on competing with new artists, 1993

> # I MISS THE COMPETITIVE PART OF [THE BUSINESS]. I'M SORRY THAT I'M NOT ALLOWED TO COMPETE. I MISS THAT.
> —MEL TILLIS, on older performers being left behind, 1994

I miss not being allowed to compete. And when country music has painted itself into this corner of "new country" or "young country," if you're not new or young, you don't qualify. . . . Eventually, I will get another shot at this. . . . My heart is saying that I have something to say.

—KENNY ROGERS, 1996

We kind of leave it up to the cosmos. . . . If you stick around long enough, you become hip again.

—DAVID BELLAMY, of the Bellamy Brothers, 1996

The life of any artist in music is five years. Well, I've been here twenty years. As Roy Acuff says, "I've seen 'em come and go, but I've never seen nobody come and stay like you have!"

—LORETTA LYNN, 1988

When Capitol Records hired Faron Young, he was 19. Hank Williams died when he was 29. Some artists may not be viable after 25 years. I guess it's over for an artist whenever the hits stop coming, when people stop buying the records. I don't know how much is a function of age and how much is a function of an artist's popularity. Maybe some of them can't change with the changing sounds. Look how long Reba has been around. She's a 21-year artist and is at her apex.

—MOON MULLINS, radio consultant, 1996

I have respect for those artists who keep making music their entire life, but I don't want to ride that downside of the bell curve. You want to be remembered at your best. You don't want to be a trivia question on some cheesy game show in 20 years and see the [contestant] get it wrong.

—GARTH BROOKS, 1996

What kind of decency is that? The man's been there 30 fuckin' years makin' them money. He paid for the son of a bitch's office that the prick sits in and lets him leave the label. Johnny Cash built the building, man.

—DWIGHT YOAKAM, on Johnny Cash's being dropped by Colombia Records, 1988

The demand is still there. I don't know who got together and decided to cut us [veteran performers] out, but they did.

—JOHNNY PAYCHECK, 1996

Dreams do come true in this business, if you wait till you're real old, like I am.
— JUNIOR BROWN, 1996

If you're not 23 years old, tight blue jeans, and a big black hat. Young and cute, you know?
— GEORGE JONES, on why his records aren't played on the radio, 1995

There's got to be a market for the older guys, based on how many people are coming to our shows. The popular wisdom is that the record-buying public isn't the same as the concert-going public. That's BS. I think it's unfair and probably illegal if you really get into it.
— EDDY RAVEN, 1996

There'll always be room for a Kitty Wells or a Loretta Lynn or a George Jones, but they'd better be good. That kind of [traditional] music won't sell anymore unless it's good. The market is dying out, shrinking on 'em.
— GLEN CAMPBELL, 1970

I was playing a date in Kerrville, Texas, not long ago, standing there in nearly waist-deep mud, singing for 100 people. A few miles away, Willie Nelson was singing for 100,000. He must know something I don't. My last album hardly sold three copies. They're warning me about it. . . . They told me I had to modernize a long time ago. I didn't believe it. I thought the old country sound would hold out.
— HANK SNOW

I knew I was in trouble the other day when I heard this guy say, "Boy, I wish they'd play some of them old guys again like Randy Travis and George Strait."
— WILLIE NELSON, 1995

I think part of the reason some people survive and prosper and get along this far, myself included, is because we wouldn't stop. I wouldn't give up on [my music]. Not even when a club owner turned on the jukebox in the middle of one of my songs, or when somebody came up to me and said, "You better play a George Strait song in the near future, *or else.*"
— HAL KETCHUM, 1996

Those [young performers] are gonna get older and the crowd's gonna get older. Somebody's got to grow up eventually. And hell, I'll ride it out. I'll be here. Eventually, a lot of these guys are gonna have to start competing with me on my terms. When all the glitter's gone, they're gonna have to start singing. And I'll be right there singing with 'em.

—MARK CHESNUTT, 1995

Country has tried [to attract] all these younger listeners. Now it's got them, but that's the most fickle demographic you can come across.

—CHARLIE DANIELS, 1996

We [old-timers] are a fact of life. Some of them, not all of them, down on Music Row act like, Johnny Cash, go away, we don't want to see you anymore. They also said that to Charlie Pride, they said that to Merle [Haggard], they said that to Waylon [Jennings], and Waylon is one of the most actively loved people in this town. Now I hear that they don't wanna play Hank Williams, Jr.'s, records, cuz he's too old.

—JOHNNY CASH, 1994

They're not playing our songs anymore, because of our age. And that's pure discrimination. . . . Us "old-timers" still have things to say. I do understand they have priorities. I used to be one of their priorities.

—WAYLON JENNINGS, 1994

We can't know where we're going until we know where we've been. And the music of the past is not just to study and put in a museum. The way to study it is to put it on the damn stereo and turn it up as loud as you can.

—EMMYLOU HARRIS, 1996

There will never be another time in country music like there is on this side of the twenty-first century, where you can still go and see Bill Monroe tonight and go see Garth Brooks and Dwight Yoakam or me or Travis Tritt tomorrow night. It's a precious time.

—MARTY STUART, 1996

MUCH TOO YOUNG (TO FEEL THIS DAMN OLD)

I can still sing as good as I ever could. But I can't sing as long. When you get older, you can't do anything as long as you once could. —MERLE HAGGARD, 1990

Where you lose it first is between the ears. —CONWAY TWITTY (1933–1993)

No two human beings remember the same experiences in the exact same way. Some call it old-timers' disease. That's when you think everybody you know is losing their memory. —WILLIE NELSON, 1988

I was lookin' for my youth. I think I wore it out. —WAYLON JENNINGS, 1996

One day you're cool, and the next you're standin' in Sears, starin' at Sans-a-Belt slacks, goin', "Man, I bet them things are comfortable!" —JEFF FOXWORTHY, comic, 1996

Age shouldn't play any part in anything. If you're still able to contribute, you should be allowed to contribute. —JOHNNY PAYCHECK, 1996

You hear people talk about midlife crisis and you cannot relate to it until you're actually there. I think the middle years are about the dissatisfaction of not having arrived at a place you thought you would, or a dream that you have not seen through. . . . You look in the mirror each day and you realize the things you thought would be there forever, such as healthy skin and hair that isn't gray, are beginning to change. Some of us yield to that very acceptingly and some of us panic. —KEITH STEGALL, 1996

By 30 you were supposed to be full grown and in command. You were either an up-and-comer, or you weren't going to make it in life. Forty was the dreaded beginning of middle age and 50 was when you finally got it all together just in time to turn 60 and die. —WILLIE NELSON, 1988

I JUST DON'T FEEL MY AGE, SO DON'T EXPECT ME TO ACT IT.

—DOTTIE WEST (1932–1991)

Almost every time, anybody who's been around for very long in our business, has some wonderful qualities, aside from what they do onstage. —MINNIE PEARL (1912–1996)

I look at it as a beginning. It's taken me so long to get where I am, I know myself and what I want, and what I don't want is to go out to pasture. I have agreed to pose nude for *Penthouse* on my one hundredth birthday. —DOLLY PARTON, on turning 50, 1996

I'm going to be 90 years old, still out there singing. They're going to have to drag me off with one of those old vaudeville hooks. —REBA McENTIRE, 1993

I'll probably be [performing] when I'm 80 years old. Probably still trying to crawl up onstage and get up behind the mike and croak out a song. —LARI WHITE, 1996

[My career is] just goin' great guns. I don't know, at 63 I'm still hangin' in there, so [I] don't need no rockin' chair, you know.

—GEORGE JONES, 1995

I have a whole lot of energy, I have very little body fat. I have a full head of hair, and I still love to sing, write, and perform. For all the reasons a young person will be in the game, I still qualify.

—HENRY PAUL, of Blackhawk, 1995

That song ["Old Hippie"] really makes you relate back to them [younger days], 'cause you wonder really how you survived it. You're damned glad you did, and you'll never do it again.

—HOWARD BELLAMY, 1996

You get to a certain point in life, you want to live long and stay around awhile. You have to start doin' different things. When you're healthy, you can do, whatever you do, you can do it better. It took me a lifetime to learn that.

—JOHNNY PAYCHECK, 1996

I still run. I still exercise. I try to undo what I did the day before.

—WILLIE NELSON, 1995

> ## EVERY TIME I GET SOMETHING FIXED, SOMETHING ELSE FALLS APART.
> —DOUG STONE, 1996

The only thing I think about is what I'm going to accomplish in the next 40 [years].

—GEORGE JONES, when asked what stands out in his 40-year career, 1995

I'm just now learning how to have an identity. I'm 27 years old and just now learning how to walk.

—WYNONNA JUDD, 1994

234~

Growing up is not being so dead set on making everybody happy.

—REBA McENTIRE, 1994

I've reached the point where I care very little what others think. I'm 40; I'm past caring.

—ROSANNE CASH, 1996

When you're 40 you can't ride the fence anymore. You gotta make definite decisions.

—DOLLY PARTON, 1986

[I've been thinking a lot about] reaching middle age and realizing that a lot of things that worked for you when you were young don't work anymore. Deciding what to take with you into the future, and what to leave behind in the past. Really stopping to care so much about what people think about you, or trying to please other people. You recover that realization that life is short, and I'm gonna do what I want to do.

—ROSANNE CASH, 1996

You get sympathy applause.

—WAYLON JENNINGS, on wearing his carpal tunnel splints onstage, 1994

If you nearly die people'll give you a standing ovation.

—DOUG STONE, survivor of three heart attacks, 1996

DEATH & DYING: ROSES ══════
IN THE SNOW

You want to be ready for it, and you want to have lived your life out and enjoyed all the life you can. And when it's through, then you want to go quietly, in sleep. That's how I want it to happen. I'm not *afraid* of dyin'. I'm afraid of the *way* I'm gonna die, you know. I'm afraid it's gonna hurt. I want it to be an easy way. So if God is listening, let me go in my sleep when I'm about a hundred years old, and I'll be happy.

—MARTY ROBBINS (1925–1982), who died at the age of 57 of a heart attack

Why complicate everything? Just let the train blow the whistle when I go. That's all I want.

—JOHNNY CASH, 1994

The last thing I said to Patsy was "I'm really going to be worried about you flying in this weather." She said, "Don't worry 'bout me. When it's my time to go, it's my time."

—DOTTIE WEST (1932–1991), on her conversation with Patsy Cline just before Patsy's fatal 1963 plane crash

The whole [airplane] looked like it'd gone through a meat grinder. You don't want to remember people lookin' like they did. You really don't. 'Cause it's with you every day of your life.

—C. B. UTHMAN, Patsy Cline search party member, 1993

The briar was so bad it had torn our clothes, and we'd been cut here and there. But we kept [searching for Patsy Cline's missing plane]. Then we came to this clearing, and I spotted the fire tower. I climbed to the top and there it was, about 20 yards away. The trees had been chewed up. Debris hung from the branches. . . . As fast as I could, I ran through the brush and the trees, and when I came up over this little rise, oh, my God, there they were. . . . [The crash site] was ghastly. The plane had crashed nose-down. It plowed into the earth on this steep hillside. . . . It was all twisted metal and pieces of bodies. There was more of Patsy's body left intact than there was of the others. It was a maddening experience.

—ROGER MILLER (1936–1992)

Somebody will write a cow-country classic about this night's ride to nowhere. Because hill folks are a sentimental lot. But the highest compliment their eulogies are likely to include is that the somber citizens who converged this day on that ugly scar in the woodland where pieces of four bodies lay, that there are real tears in their whispered words. And that they refer to each of the suddenly deceased by his or her first name.

—from Paul Harvey's news broadcast, March 6, 1963, the day Patsy Cline's fatal plane crash was discovered

I'LL NEVER LIVE TO SEE 30.

—PATSY CLINE (1932–1963), who died when she was 31

I really, truly, thought I'd caused [the crash]. Teasin' Buddy, when he told me he hoped my bus froze up, I told him, "I hope your plane crashes." And for somebody about 19 years old, a little ole country boy . . . I quit playin' music or anything.

—WAYLON JENNINGS, on the plane crash that killed Buddy Holly, 1995

[Dottie West] tried to fit 48 hours into every day. That was the big problem she had. And always running late. That's exactly what happened the night she was coming to the Opry. She was running late.

—TOMMY HILL, record producer, on Dottie West's 1991 fatal car accident, 1996

I think misery loves company. That's the [kind] of songs I wanted to sing. I had a lot of good, up-tempo, happy songs pitched to me. . . . I didn't even want to hear them. I didn't want to say anything that was short of ripping your heart out.

—REBA McENTIRE, on recording "For My Broken Heart" after the 1991 plane crash that killed seven of her band members and her road manager, 1993

Hank's family did not grieve alone.

—HOYT AXTON, on public response to the death of Hank Williams, 1996

There was a big black train that took [Jimmie Rodgers's] casket from New York City to Meridian, Mississippi. And I've been told this all my life, that on either side of the tracks, all these people, thousands of people, all the way from New York City to Meridian, would pay tribute to [him]. And when it got to Meridian, the engineer blew the low moaningest sound you ever heard from a train. That got to my mother. My mother told me that story.

—JIMMIE DALE COURT, Jimmie Rodgers's grandson, 1996

Charlie [Dick] kept the living room of Patsy's dream house locked. He left their bedroom as it was, and slept in another room. Her clothing remained in the closets. He left her makeup, hair spray, and combs in the bathroom. Friends who visited had the eerie feeling that Patsy was in the house.

—ELLIS NASSOUR, *Honky Tonk Angel: The Intimate Story of Patsy Cline*, 1993

Losing Keith made me aware of strengths I didn't know I had. . . . I'd much rather have him back and be considered a weak, wimpy ass. . . . When it comes to Keith, I'd trade all my strength to be weak again.   —LORRIE MORGAN, on the death of her husband, Keith Whitley, 1994

I watched [my father] lose his best friend. [Soon after my mother died] we were walking from the house and there's this, sitting by the door, a big picture of Mom and Dad taken about 1953, and they're sitting on an old Ford tractor. And he just walked by and laid his hand upon that picture, on her face. He said, "Drive careful," and walked out the door.

—BRION FORD, Tennessee Ernie Ford's son, on the death of his mother, 1996

I think the Boss upstairs knew we needed [Tennessee Ernie Ford] for just five minutes, and we got it. We went in to see him, and he was in his [hospital] bed with the tubes. I laid my hand on his hand, and he woke up . . . and he had been in a *coma*. His eyes blinked and he grabbed my hand. He opened his eyes. . . . I rubbed his forehead, and I said, "Hurry up. I got a boat ready and the fishing poles ready to go." He just held up his hands. That was the last I spoke to him. —BRION FORD, on his father's death, 1996

He was a fine singer, but he was also a fine man. Maybe I should've started wearing black when we lost John.
—JOHNNY CASH, on Johnny Horton's death, 1993

[Johnny] Horton, 35, died in an auto accident that was full of strange ironies. Johnny had recently married the widow of Hank Williams, who had also died in a car. Johnny played his last show at the Skyline in Austin, Texas, the same venue where Hank had given his final performance. —BOB PAXMAN, journalist, 1996

I'll miss her to pieces, but . . . I went to visit her in the nursing home a few weeks ago, and I think she's happier where she is now.
—REBA McENTIRE, on Minnie Pearl's death, 1996

I can just imagine the smile on God's face when [Minnie Pearl] shows up in heaven sayin', "How*dy*! I'm just so proud to be here!"
—DOLLY PARTON, 1996

[Minnie Pearl's] death is going to pull a little bit of the guts out of [Nashville]. —RALPH EMERY, radio personality and host of *Nashville Now*, 1996

I WONDER IF I COULD TALK RIGHT BACK THEN?

—MEL TILLIS, on what he might have been like in a past life, 1988

Once you're [dead], you're beloved. Y'know, the "late, great," and "what he did for our music." But until then, it's always, "trouble-makin' son of a bitch." —WAYLON JENNINGS, 1975

Most everybody had written me off. Oh yeah, they all acted like they were proud of me when I straightened up. Some of them are still mad about it though, 'cause I didn't go ahead and die so they'd have a legend to sing about and put in Hillbilly Heaven. —JOHNNY CASH, 1988

A lot of people had her gone, you know. A lot of people had me gone for a while there, too. —GEORGE JONES, on Tammy Wynette's recent health problems, 1995

I would like to paraphrase Mark Twain; "Rumors of my impending death are greatly exaggerated." —TAMMY WYNETTE, 1996

You don't appreciate home till you leave it and, let me tell you, you can't appreciate life till you've almost left it. Some hope and die with their song still in them. . . . This ole gal used to think happiness resulted when my earnings matched my yearnings. Not anymore. —PATSY CLINE (1932–1963), after her near-fatal car crash

I was a totally different person. I talked about Barbara Mandrell in the third person. That was *her*. —BARBARA MANDRELL, on recovering from her 1984 near-fatal car crash, 1996

I have to figure I'm probably about where I belong in life for the way I've treated it [my body]. I was pushin' it; I forgot how old I was. And I couldn't live climbin' those walls forever, havin' a good time. —HOYT AXTON, on his 1995 stroke, 1996

My close calls with death have taught me to embrace life even more intensely. I don't sleep too many days away anymore. It's refocused what's important—my family, my music, and enjoying life. . . . If it all ended today, I'd have to say I've had a good time. It's been a lot of fun.   —JOHN BERRY, 1996

When I sing a song, I want to make it sound like the last thing I ever say in my life.   —LEFTY FRIZZELL'S last words (1928–1975)

I ain't worried about dying. I'm worried about living.

—DOUG STONE

SOURCES

BOOKS

Biracree, Tom. *The Country Music Almanac.* New York: Prentice Hall, 1993.

Cunniff, Albert. *Waylon Jennings.* New York: Kensington, 1985.

Emery, Ralph, and Tom Carter. *Memories: The Autobiography of Ralph Emery.* New York: Pocket Books, 1992.

Faragher, Scott. *Music City Babylon.* New York: Birch Lane, 1992.

Haggard, Merle, and Peggy Russell. *Sing Me Back Home.* New York: Times Books, 1981.

Horstman, Dorothy. *Sing Your Heart Out, Country Boy.* Nashville: Country Music Foundation Press, 1996.

Lynn, Loretta, and George Vecsey. *Coal Miner's Daughter.* New York: Warner, 1976.

Malone, Bill C. *Country Music, U.S.A.* Austin: University of Texas Press, 1968.

Nash, Alanna. *Behind Closed Doors: Talking With the Legends of Country Music.* New York: Knopf, 1988.

Nassour, Ellis. *Honky Tonk Angel: The Intimate Story of Patsy Cline.* New York: St. Martin's Press, 1993.

Nelson, Willie, and Bud Shrake. *Willie.* New York: Simon & Schuster, 1988.

Oermann, Robert K. *America's Music: The Roots of Country.* Atlanta: Turner, 1996.

Oermann, Robert K., and Mary Bufwack. *Finding Her Voice: The Saga of Women in Country Music.* New York: Crown, 1993.

Riese, Randall. *Nashville Babylon.* New York: Congdon & Weed, 1988.

Tillis, Mel, and Walter Wager. *Stutterin' Boy.* New York: Rawson, 1985.

Tritt, Travis. *Ten Feet Tall and Bulletproof.* New York: Warner, 1995.

Williams, Roger M. *Sing a Sad Song: The Life of Hank Williams.* New York: Ballantine Books, 1970.

MAGAZINES AND NEWSPAPERS

Cosmopolitan

Country America

Country Music

Country Weekly

Esquire

Guitar Player

Ladies Home Journal

Los Angeles Times

Modern Screen's Country Music

New Country

Orange County Register

People

Playboy

Rolling Stone

TV Guide

Vogue

Working Woman

TELEVISION

At the Ryman. TNN, Nashville. January–June 1996.

Country News, TNN, Nashville, January–June 1996.

Exclusively Leeza (with Robert Reynolds and Trisha Yearwood). TNN, Nashville. February 13, 1996.

Full Access: On Tour with Travis Tritt. TNN, Nashville. May 9, 1996.

Life and Times of Bill Monroe. TNN, Nashville. March 7, 1996.

Life and Times of Bob Wills. TNN, Nashville. March 14, 1996.

Life and Times of Conway Twitty. TNN, Nashville. November 15, 1995.

Life and Times of Dottie West. TNN, Nashville. February 27, 1996.

Life and Times of Ernest Tubb. TNN, Nashville. February 22, 1996.

Life and Times of the Everly Brothers. TNN, Nashville. March 21, 1996.

Life and Times of Hank Williams. TNN, Nashville. January 12, 1996.

Life and Times of Kenny Rogers. TNN, Nashville. May 2, 1996.

Life and Times of Lefty Frizzell. TNN, Nashville. March 28, 1996.

Life and Times of Marty Robbins. TNN, Nashville. January 14, 1996.

Life and Times of Minnie Pearl. TNN, Nashville. February 15, 1996.

Life and Times of Roy Acuff. TNN. Nashville. January 18, 1996.

Life and Times of Tennessee Ernie Ford. TNN, Nashville. February 8, 1996.

Loretta Lynn: The Seasons of My Life. TNN, Nashville. May 15, 1996.

Martina McBride: Full Speed Ahead (with Garth Brooks). TNN, Nashville. February 20, 1996.

Merle Haggard: An American Story. TNN, Nashville. May 13–14, 1996.

Monday Night Concerts (with Sawyer Brown, Mac McAnnally, Pam Tillis, and Kim Richey). TNN, Nashville. April 29, 1996.

Music City Tonight. TNN, Nashville. November–January 1995–96.

Not Fade Away: Remembering Buddy Holly. TNN, Nashville. February 5, 1996.

Phyliss George (with Jeff Foxworthy). TNN, Nashville. February 27, 1996.

Ralph Emery: On the Record (with Brooks & Dunn). TNN, Nashville. January 1996.

The Road. TNN, Nashville. January–June 1996.

Soulmates (with Denise Jackson, Janine Dunn, and June Carter Cash). TNN, Nashville. April 30, 1996.